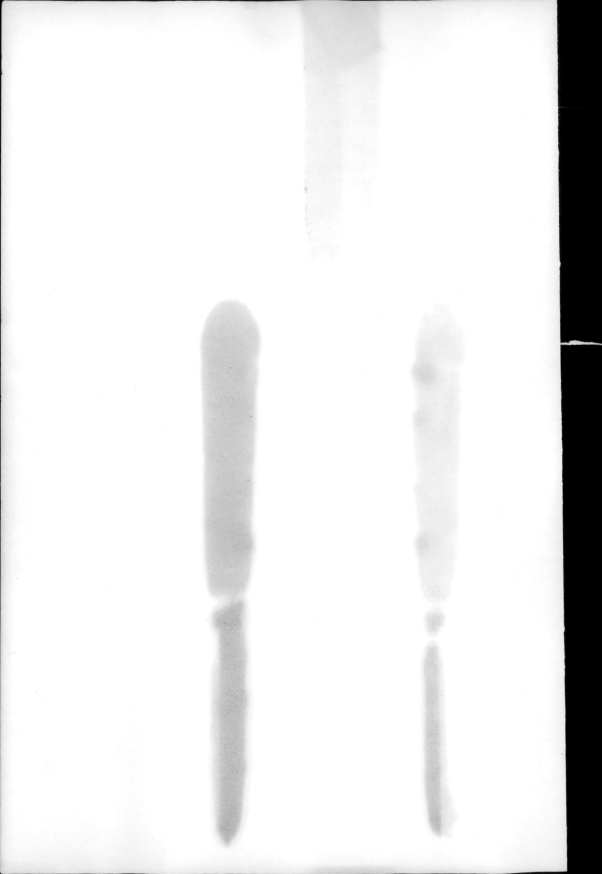

WATCHING
THE WILD APES

WATCHING

E. P. Dutton & Co., Inc.   New York

THE WILD APES

The Primate Studies of
Goodall, Fossey, and Galdikas

by Bettyann Kevles

Title page photograph: From left to right,
infant gorilla, chimpanzee, and orangutan at the
Los Angeles Zoo.

Photographs on page 51 (both) and page 52 (top) are
from *In the Shadow of Man* by Jane Van Lawick-Goodall,
copyright © 1971 by Hugo and Jane Van Lawick-Goodall.
Reprinted by permission of the publisher, Houghton
Mifflin Company, Boston.

LIBRARY OF CONGRESS CATALOGING IN PUBLICATION DATA

Kevles, Bettyann Holtzmann   Watching the wild apes

SUMMARY: Describes the field work of three primatologists
and what their studies have revealed about the behavioral
patterns of chimpanzees, gorillas, and orangutans in their
natural habitat.

1. Apes—Behavior—Juvenile literature.   2. Goodall, Jane—
Juvenile literature.   3. Fossey, Dian—Juvenile literature.
4. Galdikas, Biruté—Juvenile literature.
[1.   Apes—Habits and behavior.   2.   Goodall, Jane.
3.   Fossey, Dian.   4.   Galdikas, Biruté]   I. Title.

QL737.P96K4   599'.884'045   75–38939   ISBN 0–525–42233–1

Published simultaneously in Canada by Clarke,
Irwin & Company Limited, Toronto and Vancouver

Designed by Meri Shardin
Printed in the U.S.A.   First Edition
10   9   8   7   6   5   4   3   2   1

For Daniel, Beth, and Jonathan

ACKNOWLEDGMENTS

Many individuals gave generously of their time and knowledge to help me complete this book. I became interested in the study of primatology through the lecture series sponsored by the L. S. B. Leakey Foundation. I am very grateful to Dr. Edwin S. Munger, president of the foundation, who encouraged and helped me enthusiastically from vision to completion. When the project was under way, Dr. David Hamburg steered me through the scientific materials and remained a sympathetic guide, critic, and sounding board, especially with reference to the chimpanzee material.

Dr. Patrick McGinnis of the Stanford Outdoor Primate Facility graciously showed me around that installation. Also at Stanford, the many Gombe alumni were most helpful, especially Donna Marie Anderson.

Dr. William D'Arcy at the Missouri Botanical Gardens provided vivid material about the Virunga volcanoes and pointed out the interrelatedness of the many scientific disciplines that cooperate in primate research. Julie Webb discussed her own work with gorillas, and Alan O'Brien helped verify the description of Dian Fossey.

I am grateful to Dr. Peter Rodman for his insights into orangutan behavior and life on Borneo. I want especially to thank Biruté Galdikas, the only member of this trio of scientists who was in the United States while I was writing. She responded wholeheartedly to all my questions and brought a sense of immediacy to the research.

Dr. Alan Walker at Harvard's Peabody Museum kindly provided the correct taxonomic terminology.

I wish to express my appreciation to the Greater Los Angeles Zoo Association for arranging a tour of their facilities. Florence Patagalia, librarian at the Westridge School, and Jeanne Tatrow, at the Millikan Library at the California Institute of Technology, were tremendously helpful in tracking down information. I want to thank Edith Taylor and Marlene Thick and Rita Pearson for their help typing the manuscript. My editor, Susan Shapiro, has shared my fascination with the wild apes and I am grateful to her for expert guidance all along the way. And, finally, I am indebted to Daniel Kevles, my husband, for his constant enthusiasm and support.

Author's Note

The events described in Chapters 2, 6, and 9 arc imaginative re-constructions of days in the lives of the great apes. The animals are real, and the events have happened, but not necessarily in the order described and not in so short a period of time.

Contents

Maps appear on pages 21, 77, and 117.
Photographs appear on pages 7–9, 16,
51–54, 68, 93–95, 110, and 131–133.

A New Look

A dark-haired American scientist crouched low in the lush African foliage, her left hand drawn near her mouth, her right hand extended palm upward among the thick leaves. Nearby a giant wild gorilla gazed down upon the hand, so like its own. Then, hesitantly, it stepped closer and brushed the human fingers. This unprecedented "handshake" symbolizes the newest chapter in the story of primatology, the study of our nearest relative, the great ape.

The story began at least 5 million years ago, when thick, humid forests, dark in primeval growth, covered the earth. As life evolved, it culminated at one moment in evolutionary time in an anthropoid creature somewhere between today's great apes and *Homo sapiens*. This hominoid left two streams of descendants, one of which, the great apes, continued living and changing within the forests, while the other, early humans, quit the fruit-laden trees to evolve into a very separate animal.

Millennia passed. The glacial epochs left the earth cooled down and flooded. The rain forests were gradually pressed into a few tropical areas in the Pacific, in Africa, and in South America. The apes clung to the trees and swamps that sheltered them, gradually adapting themselves as the forests changed, unmindful of that other animal who looked so much like themselves—*Homo sapien*.

1

Throughout the ages of recorded history, great apes and humans lived side by side in the tropical forests of Africa and Asia, but they seldom met. Apes avoided man the hunter. And men avoided the apes, wary of traits that they superstitiously projected onto the animals from their own folk mythologies and nightmares.

Fear colored the fantasies that Africans and Malayans told about these creatures. Fear, and a conviction that apes looked much too human not to have once been human beings. Malayans explained to a Dutch traveler in the seventeenth century that the long-haired red orangutans in the forests of Sumatra and Borneo had once been people, arrogant people who had blasphemed the gods and had as punishment been transformed into beasts.

Halfway around the world at the same time, Africans scorned the giant black gorillas that roamed the wooded mountain slopes as once lazy villagers, people who had refused to work and wandered away into the jungle where, little by little, they had forgotten the ways of people and reverted to animals. Some Africans today still refuse to hunt the brown chimpanzees—they call the smaller apes half brothers, too close to use for food, but still not human.

Undisturbed by these stories that humans told, these tailless great apes—orangutans, gorillas, and chimpanzees—foraged the dark forests for their food and built themselves soft nests each night to sleep in. Their lives were not yet threatened by their hairless cousins who stood erect and cut down the life-giving trees.

Soon explorers and traders penetrated the forest sanctuaries, bringing home weird stories of half-human monsters. The Europeans believed these yarns. After all, had they not populated their own forests with werewolves and satyrs? French and Portuguese sailors eagerly lapped up and then repeated horror stories of apes who murdered, pillaged, and even ravaged human females.

The skeptical eighteenth-century public in Europe demanded proof of these sailors' boasts. The sailors obliged by kidnapping tiny animals, usually infant chimpanzees, but sometimes a baby gorilla or orangutan. Taken from their forest homes, the frightened orphans suffered ocean crossings in order to appear at court, decked out in preposterous costumes to please a king. Orphanhood, the ordeal of the sea, and Europe's cold winters were too much for them. They usually died within a year.

They left their skin and skeletal remains far from their native swamps and vines to be examined by a curious new human breed—the collector. Their final resting places were glass cases in the private museums that had sprung up throughout Europe during the eighteenth century.

Some of these collectors blossomed into scientists who stuffed the lifeless skins and compared and measured sets of skulls, and arm and leg bones. They even tried to sort out the three great apes, one from the other, to make sense out of the fascinating new wealth of animal life that arrived with each ship from the Far East and Africa.

Pre-eminent among these scientists, the Swedish doctor Linnaeus managed to fit the great jumble of discoveries into a framework. He arranged the animal kingdom into categories, and the categories into subcategories, and again into even smaller groups. When he reached Primate, he did not hesitate to group the apes together with man in the same order. Since his time scientists have regrouped many of the other animals, and even today they disagree as to what goes where. But all agree with Linnaeus that the Primate superfamily Hominoidea contains three families: Hylobatidae, the gibbons; Hominidae, whose only living specie is *Homo sapien;* and Pongidae, which has three living representatives—*Pan,* which includes chimpanzees and gorillas, and *Pongo,* only the orangutans.

Linnaeus's classifications were the starting point for Charles Darwin's theory of evolution. Darwin explained the haunting similarity between ourselves and the apes as a family resemblance. We look alike because we are alike and share a common ancestor. This insight of Darwin's revolutionized man's vision of his own place in natural history. At the same time it increased the status of the apes in the eyes of some people. But Darwin's "heresy" fomented riots by some and stirred deep anxiety in the hearts of others. They did not want to be related to such "brutes."

Many nineteenth-century people saw the apes as just that—brutes. This vision of bloodthirsty giants lusting after human flesh was exploited by a French-American explorer, Paul du Chaillu. He was a young charlatan who convinced the Boston Academy of Natural Sciences to send him on an expensive expedition to his native Gabon in East Africa to search out wild gorillas. Four years and two thousand walking miles later, Du Chaillu published a very popular account of his adventures. He claimed that gorillas had threatened him repeatedly and that he had seen them engaged in beastly pastimes. He did not mention that they usually ran whenever they saw Du Chaillu's party coming, nor that the great "brute" he captured was a year-old infant who pined away and died after the hunters had killed his mother. Hindsight reveals that Du Chaillu "borrowed" some of his "on-the-spot" illustrations from the archives of the British Museum. But he did, in fact, go into the wilderness to try to find gorillas. And in so doing, Du Chaillu became the first modern field primatologist.

A field primatologist describes animals as they live in their natural habitats the way an anthropologist studies the patterns of life in sometimes remote human communities. Some primatologists are anthropologists, some are zoologists. Most agree that although the great apes are remarkably complex in the way they live, they do not have a culture—a body of tradition that they pass on from one generation to another—which characterizes all human societies.

Du Chaillu's outlandish exaggerations built up an audience interested in great apes and affected a whole generation of scientists. Among them was Richard L. Garner from Harvard University. He had spent some time at New York's Central Park Zoo, read Du Chaillu, and set out for Africa anyway, in 1893—utterly terrified of the animals he planned to watch.

Garner was a cautious man. When he reached West Africa he

had a metal cage built, painted it green, and brought it into the forest. There he climbed inside with his kerosene stove and camp bed. He waited, notebook in hand, for 112 days and nights, for the chimpanzees and gorillas to come to him. His stationary circumstances certainly limited his observations, yet he honestly recorded what he heard and what he did *not* see. Garner noted that he never witnessed any ferocious or aggressive behavior, except for one strange wild dance during a rainstorm that he called a "carnival." It was a tale so bizarre that most scientists who read the account rejected it as a hallucination brought on by isolation in the jungle. Ironically, later observers have also seen Garner's "vision."

Meanwhile, apes continued to forage, and sleep, and raise their infants in the rain forests, as more and more humans invaded their ranges. Many amateur naturalists took up primate-watching early in the twentieth century, making excursions into the forests with field glasses and cameras. But the more serious primatologists took a different tack. They captured live apes and transported those that managed to survive to private primate colonies on the semitropical islands of Tenerife, near Spain, and Cuba, off the coast of Florida.

The American Museum of Natural History in New York sent the sculptor-scientist Carl Akeley to the Congo in 1921, where he died five years later, but not before convincing the Belgian authorities to turn the area into a park to protect the gorillas. But his death put an end to research there for yet another decade.

At about the same time another American, Robert Yerkes, a psychologist from Yale University, was reshaping the course of primatology away from the forests by establishing a huge primate colony within the United States. In his laboratory, first set up in New Haven, Connecticut, and later moved to Orange Park, Florida, Yerkes gathered together healthy apes and managed to breed them in captivity. He then used the great apes as stand-ins for humans in a great variety of medical and psychological experiments. Yerkes also pitted the three great apes against each other in tests he devised to rank them in intelligence—that is, intelligence according to human standards. Yerkes learned a great deal about the ways that captive animals can be raised and trained, and he also learned how the great apes compare with humans. But the Yerkes people could not understand the apes as successful animals in terms of the way they had adapted to their own forest habitats. Because they had never been able to observe apes in their natural settings, they found some ape behavior incomprehensible.

As the infant orangutan clings to its mother's body hair as she moves slowly through the forest, so in captivity, a newborn chimpanzee, removed from its mother, still clings desperately to a metal bar, a wooden beam, to anything available. But why apes have this clinging instinct the primatologist could not explain.

Yerkes realized that he would have to know something about how the great apes lived in nature to make more sense of what they did in the laboratory. But the prospect of finding volunteers to go into the remote rain forests of Africa and Asia to observe these animals seemed overwhelmingly complicated in the economic climate of the 1930s Depression.

Yerkes sent several observers into the forests, but only one was successful, a remarkable scientist who worked not with the chimpanzee and gorilla, but with a smaller primate, the howler monkey. C. R. Carpenter, then a young zoologist from Harvard, went to Panama in 1934 and spent several months among these monkeys, getting them used to him so that after a while they behaved as if he were another part of the scenery. Carpenter's work with these monkeys, and then in 1938 his similar study of the siamangs in Thailand, really began a new approach to studying primates. This is what is now called the ethology of primates, the study of their behavior in the wild. Other scientists, like the Nobel Prize winner Konrad Lorenz, had been studying the ethology of birds and fish. Now Carpenter introduced this careful kind of observation to the smaller primates. But he did not try to approach the great apes in this way. They seemed more elusive, more dangerous, and much harder to reach in their remote strongholds near the equator.

All this time, the apes in their forests were being ruthlessly hunted down by black-marketeering animal dealers. With the exception of men like Akeley and Carpenter, the apes were ignored by scientists. Finally, after World War II, a group of primatologists appeared who were interested in studying the great apes in their own environments.

The man who initiated much of this new work was the late Louis S. B. Leakey. A self-taught anthropologist from Kenya, who eventually won degrees from Cambridge University, Leakey was a stubborn maverick who spent his life seeking fossil evidence in the wilderness to prove that Africa is mankind's birthplace.

Leakey moved from one inspired hunch to the next. By 1957 he was the curator of the Coryndon Museum in Nairobi, Kenya, and with his wife, Mary, had settled into an annual trip to dig in the Olduvai Gorge, a site remote in Tanzania's Serengeti Plain. A geological miracle, the Gorge exposes rugged layers of earth as if someone had sliced into the crust with a cake knife and turned it over, providing a cross section of our geological past.

Paul du Chaillu shooting a gorilla in Africa.

From *Africa* (1861)
by Paul du Chaillu

Safe in his cage, Richard Garner observes, and is observed by, some wild chimpanzees in Africa.

Below, a chimpanzee rain dance or "carnival" as described by Garner.

From *Apes and Monkeys* (1900)
by R. L. Garner

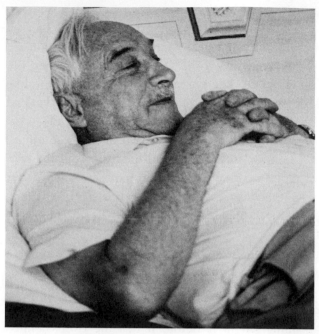

Louis S. B. Leakey in his later years.

The Leakeys had been digging at a particular site in the Gorge for some time, where they found animal fossils as well as the stone tools left by early hominids. A few years later Mary Leakey uncovered an almost complete skull that Louis had long believed must exist there. He nicknamed that skull "nutcracker man" because of its huge molars. In 1957, however, they had not yet discovered *Zinjanthropus,* but had found the living site complete with man-made stone chips and fossil remains of other animals—the food of early man, perhaps—which said something about the kind of lives our predecessors led. (Since the Leakeys' discovery, this skull has been reclassified in the general category of *Australopithecus.*)

That year, when the Leakeys again set out for Olduvai, they brought with them Leakey's new assistant secretary from the museum in Nairobi, a young Englishwoman, Jane Goodall. An animal lover, she had come to Africa to meet its wildlife. She arrived at the Gorge during the long dry season when the rocks sheltered miniature antelopes no larger than an English hare.

Watching the rare animals as they scrounged for food among the dry stones, Leakey discussed the site of the dig with her. He explained that eons ago the side gorge had followed the shoreline of an early Pleistocene lake, and that the food fossils he had found showed that Pleistocene man had camped near the lakeshore, perhaps depending on the lake for food and protection.

As he went on talking, Leakey seemed to stray from his subject. He thought aloud about the wild chimpanzees that wander out of the forests to congregate on the shores of Lake Tanganyika. Noisy and busy, they scurry for cover whenever humans appear. But if the chimps could get used to humans, Leakey guessed, if a human observer could find out how they behave as a social unit, the knowledge might tell us about the social behavior of early humans. Ethology, especially primate ethology, was still a new science in 1957, and Leakey liked the idea of one of his protégés getting immersed in it before it became overwhelmed with researchers and technicalities.

Of course, Leakey added, any research done on chimpanzees would be difficult. People had already tried it; he had sent a young man years before who had given up after six months. Lake Tanganyika, though beautiful, is harsh, wild, and remote. Whoever tried to do field work there would have to be someone of special dedication and patience. Most likely it would take years—who could say how many—to get the chimpanzees habituated to humans. But if it could be done, Leakey predicted, it would prove immensely rewarding.

When Leakey completed his description of this remarkable "someone," he turned to Jane Goodall and suggested that she was the person.

Flattered and also bewildered, Jane Goodall accepted the challenge. She was untrained then, and carefree, ready to try something different. But it took three years before she set out for the proposed campsite on the Gombe Stream with her mother, Vanne Goodall, at her side. Together they encountered tropical fevers, cruel terrain, and wild animals of all descriptions, including chimpanzees.

What she has learned since 1960 has proven as scientifically rewarding as Leakey predicted. Primate ethology has now grown into a major science, sending shock waves of excitement into related fields. Anthropologists concerned with human evolution are more than ever convinced of the closeness of human prehistory to that of the apes. Their convictions have been reinforced by the findings of biochemists and geneticists, who have found similarities between human and chimpanzee chromosomes, blood types, and enzymes. Darwin was uncannily correct.

The great apes have hands that can grasp. Their eyes move together in binocular vision that enables them to see in depth. And, like humans, apes rely so much on seeing that they have lost the greater sense of smell and rely on sight more than scent to detect danger. Their hemoglobin is identical to ours and, in fact, they share our physiology so much that they succumb to the same diseases, especially intestinal troubles and lung infections. At Gombe, the chimps suffered horribly in 1967 from a polio epidemic.

Jane Goodall's camp on the shores of the Gombe Stream was still remote, but far from lonely by the mid-1970s. Students and visitors came to help her with her work. Unlike some earlier primatologists, such as Garner, who looked upon apes as an inferior species, failed competitors in the evolutionary race, these modern primatologists respect the apes for their unique qualities as animals.

Delighted with the success of the chimpanzee project, Leakey moved on to a second plan. He wanted to find someone to do the same kind of study on the vanishing mountain gorilla. Shy of men, the gorillas hide from humans, often indulging in some heavy chest-poundings as they go. They fear man because man has hunted them and whittled down their home ranges, forcing a retreat into the barely passable volcanic mountaintops of Central Africa.

Far from these mountains, in Louisville, Kentucky, Dian Fossey, an occupational therapist, had been nourishing a lifelong interest in gorillas. When she managed to save up enough money to visit Africa, she sought out the mountain gorillas. Louis Leakey later heard about her and sought *her* out. Recognizing Fossey at once as a possible candidate for the difficult project, he helped her to get started.

Dian Fossey began her new life in the misty volcanic rain forests in 1966. Alone, cautious, and patient, she habituated the gorillas and got them so used to her that in 1970 the giant male, Peanuts, honored her with that famous "handshake." Since then Dian Fossey has continued developing a very personal approach, and she has destroyed the ancient gorilla myths.

Gorillas are threatened, and so are the orangutans, the only Asian member of the great apes. The orangutan is different from the African apes in many ways. Its ancestors separated from the common pongid ancestor millions of years ago and it has adapted to a quite different habitat. For centuries a veil of mystery surrounded the huge red ape. Solitary by nature, and much more arboreal, the orangutans are hard to understand. But with the African projects doing so well, Leakey sought out one more candidate to study the missing corner of the ape triangle. He found her while he was lecturing at UCLA, in the anthropologist Biruté Galdikas-Brindamour.

Capable and determined, Biruté Galdikas set off for Indonesia with her husband, Rod Brindamour, in 1971. After flying from one island to another, they reached their steaming campsite near the equator in Kalimantan Province in Indonesian Borneo, the historic island of the head-hunters. In 1975, after four years, Biruté Galdikas had managed to penetrate some of the mystery shrouding the remarkable orangutan.

The orangutan differs from the gorilla, and the gorilla from the chimpanzee, as the forests they inhabit differ from each other. Sadly, both the forests and the apes they shelter are threatened as never before by encroaching civilization—the hunter, the logger, and the farmer. The great apes, once safely remote from *Homo sapiens,* now live dependent on the solicitude of human benefactors.

The threat adds urgency to these field studies. Most probably the kind of work that Jane Goodall, Dian Fossey, and Biruté Galdikas have been doing can be done only once, and that once is now. These studies differ in depth from the many short-term projects that other primatologists have tried. And at the very least these apes have found champions.

These women are totally dedicated to their subjects. They carefully record the lives of the apes and at the same time they are campaigning to save them from extinction as wild species. Each one is prepared to spend many years (fifteen already in the case of Goodall) observing in great detail the lives of individual animals, their families, and the larger social group. Each has devised individual techniques to advance her work, depending on her instincts and developing sophistication as a scientist. And each woman's personality colors the mood of her camp.

The work progresses. Increasingly the primatologists share results—comparing, contrasting, and always stimulating more questions that need more answers. Their laboratories are the forests. Here they live and work among their subjects—the wild apes.

PART I

CHIMPANZEES

Jane Goodall treats a wild chimpanzee to bananas near her campsite at the Gombe Stream.

1

Jane Goodall
in Tanzania

Clear water lapped the sandy shores of Lake Tanganyika where the baboons congregated, protected by game scouts in the Gombe Stream Reserve. The lake was mirror-bright in the summer calm that July day in 1960. But fishing boats clung to the shores, wary of sudden winds that could raise whitecaps, making the fresh-water lake seem like an ocean. Beyond the beach at Gombe, the shoreline zigzagged through rocky coves until sixteen miles to the south the port town of Kigoma thrust quays and jetties into the waters. Kigoma's shops, post office, and telegraph linked Gombe with the rest of Tanzania. Northward along the eastern shore of Lake Tanganyika were the new nations of Burundi and Rwanda. And to the west, thirty miles across the lake, the Belgian Congo was just becoming the independent nation of Zaire.

Jane Goodall was twenty-six years old when she first saw Lake Tanganyika, and she was in a hurry. Almost three years had slipped by since Louis Leakey first proposed the chimpanzee research. She had spent the time, reluctantly, in London. And while she studied primate zoology at the Royal Free Hospital and the London Zoo, Louis Leakey searched for someone to finance her project.

It seemed that she had spent the first twenty-three years of her life waiting to reach Africa the first time. Even as a small child in Bournemouth, England, animals had fascinated her, and she had written up careful descriptions of the local birds. Her school years in London were filled with zoo visits, and she vowed then to visit Africa, where these animals lived uncaged. After high school Goodall took secretarial courses and with these skills presented herself at the Coryndon Museum in Nairobi. Since 1957 she had seen many wild animals at Olduvai and elsewhere. Now she was waiting to study them.

East Africa still seethed in 1960 as civil war raged in the Congo. In what was then Tanganyika, the British had relinquished their control and the new authorities refused to allow a woman, a young white woman, to enter the bush alone. Finally Goodall's mother, Vanne Morris Goodall, agreed to go along for the first few months. That settled, she had to wait again as new difficulties erupted among the fishermen on the lake. But at least she was waiting in Africa now, and Leakey arranged for her to spend three weeks on an uninhabited island in the middle of Lake Victoria, practicing monkey-watching.

From Lolui Island the women at last went to Nairobi, Kenya. Then they drove eight hundred miles westward over rugged roads through Tanganyika to the lakeside city of Kigoma, which was jammed with Belgian refugees from the Congo. The fighting there was frightfully real, but infinitely remote from the lives of the chimpanzees at Gombe. Fifteen years later, however, in 1975, the specter of that civil war reappeared, threatening Goodall's chimpanzee research.

But that was a long way off from the July day in 1960 when the park ranger's launch deposited the Goodalls on the ten-mile strip of beach, part of the game preserve that had been set aside by the British in 1923 as a haven for wild apes. Jane Goodall had noticed as they approached how most of the hillsides along the lake were dry and eroded. But when they reached the thirty square miles of the preserve, the scenery turned green. The protected mountains were rich in lush forests that from the boat, at least, seemed absolutely impenetrable.

Gombe still felt unreal to her, even as she helped unload their crates and boxes from the boat. As if to prove that she had really arrived, she left the ranger, her mother, and Dominic, the cook she had hired in Kigoma, and plunged headlong into the foliage and scrambled up the hillside. When she returned, scratched and filthy, she felt she had begun to know the terrain.

Even in those scorching days, when the temperature topped 100° F., the Gombe Stream Reserve was beautiful. The whole park is an ecological mosaic, from the hills rising abruptly near the beach, itself two thousand feet above sea level, to the mountains five thousand feet high. The hills and valleys between them are covered with gallery rain forest where trees rise eighty feet and the deep undergrowth is rich in vines and brilliant flowers. There is open woodland on the upper slopes, but only tall grass grows on the peaks and ridges. Even in the dry season, scores of freshwater streams break over waterfalls, rushing to meet the seemingly bottomless lake.

Here, in this remnant of the primeval forest belt that once crossed all of Central Africa, the longhaired Gombe chimpanzee, *Pan troglodytes schweinfurthii,* lives alongside wild bush pigs, bushbuck, baboons, and occasional buffalo. Predator snakes and leopards seldom bother them, and they are protected by law from their worst enemy, man.

That summer the human population at Gombe included the two Goodalls in their tent near the beach; Dominic with his wife and daughter in another tent nearer the water; and, on the beach itself, well within earshot, two park scouts and the headman of the Kasekela village, local fishermen who were allowed to use the beach during the summer to dry their catch. That was all.

The Africans who guided Goodall through the forest for the first few days soon left. But not before they had taught her some crucial lessons: how to follow the smooth trails that the baboons and pigs had made so she did not have to break new paths into the dense bush, how to cross the swift streams and, above all, how to spot the red and orange fruit of the *msulula* tree, a favorite of the chimpanzees. The guides watched with her from a grassy clearing on another slope as sixteen chimpanzees climbed into the thick branches to eat.

After ten days the chimpanzees left that msulula tree. For the next eight weeks after her guides had gone, Goodall sought out other apes, hoping to meet them and watch them from a closer vantage point. As time passed, she grew to know her way around the valleys, especially the three nearest her camp that she named the Home Valley, the Pocket, and Mlinda. The baboon trails became as familiar to her as London's streets, and the cicada's call like the din of traffic.

But Gombe was not a city park. Its harsh beauty hid booby traps—sleeping leopards that would attack if wakened, and Cape buffalo that charge viciously, their heads up high until, at the last moment, they lower them to gore their victims. And the clear waters of the lake, free from the deadly bilharzia snail that poisons so many of the other African lakes, housed the water cobra for whose bite, then, there was no serum cure.

Both luck and instinct helped her survive these threats. She moved slowly, and remained still when, standing in the lake, a wave deposited a cobra on her foot, or when in the bush she came upon a sleeping buffalo.

Goodall crisscrossed the valleys and the hills every day, looking for chimpanzees. After her ten-day watch of the msulula tree, she did not see any chimps at all, and when she heard their fearsome *hoos,* the sounds began to taunt her. If she did glimpse a chimp, it fled instantly. She despaired at ever accomplishing her goal.

Meanwhile, her meager supply of funds drained out. Leakey's sponsor had supplied her with a motorboat, a tent, and enough money to keep her project going for three months. After two months she had made slim progress. Then another forest demon struck both women at the same time.

A Kigoma doctor had told them not to worry about malaria, that there was none in the area. So neither had taken any preventive medicine. Now fever felled them, and they lay side by side in their tent on camp beds. Each day when Goodall drew the thermometer from her mother's lips, it read 105° F. She felt too weak even to risk the boat ride to Kigoma as Dominic urged. Instead they gratefully accepted the sweets he concocted to make them eat as he hovered close by, fearful for their lives.

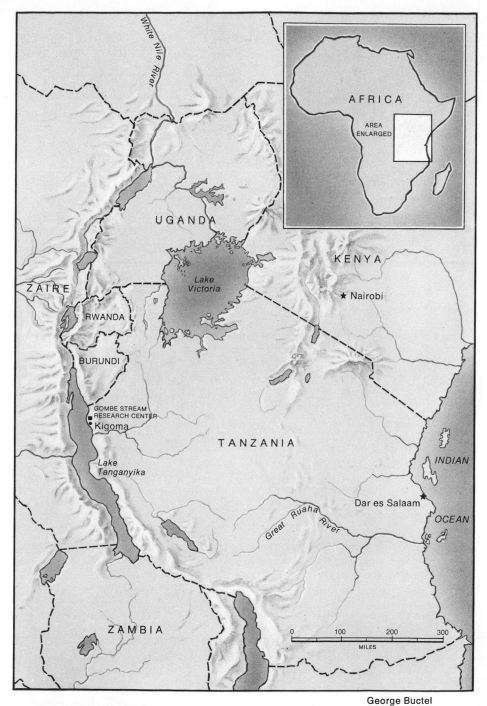

White Nile River

AFRICA

AREA
ENLARGED

UGANDA

KENYA

ZAIRE

Lake
Victoria

★ Nairobi

RWANDA

BURUNDI

GOMBE STREAM
RESEARCH CENTER
■ Kigoma

TANZANIA

INDIAN

Lake
Tanganyika

Great Ruaha River

Dar es Salaam

OCEAN

ZAMBIA

0   100   200   300
MILES

George Buctel

Gombe Stream Research Center in Tanzania

Naturally thin, but now almost bony from dehydration, the young woman awoke one morning with her fever gone and left the tent. She went up the steep slope, back to her mission. Dawn had not yet broken as she climbed, feeling panic at the thought of so much lost time. She was weak from the sudden exertion and paused occasionally until she reached an open space. Here she stopped and saw that she was on a peak about a thousand feet above the lake. Dawn had beaten her to the mountaintop and she could see the clear waters and the white ribbon of sand below. Somewhere down there the fishermen might be preparing their nets to swoop up the sardine-like *dagaa*. Directly below her stood the tent, protecting her still feverish mother from the sun. She turned slowly, scanning the panorama. Binoculars to her eyes, she began searching the Home Valley for chimpanzees.

Across from where she crouched on the peak, a deep ravine separated her from another slope. And there, where a grove of fig trees were in fruit, she noticed first a movement and then she saw three chimpanzees—standing and staring at her. She waited for them to vanish as they always had. But this time they ambled along toward the fig trees and began to forage. They were no more than eighty yards away from her, much closer than she had yet been to any wild chimpanzees. She spent that whole day up there, conspicuous on the rocky peak. Other chimps joined the first three feasting on the sweet fruit. They saw her but ignored her. She did not threaten them with her slow, deliberate movements. Soon they accepted her strange but harmless presence near them.

That night Goodall scrambled down the slope and excitedly related the good news. Her exhilaration may have proved contagious, for soon her mother's fever broke. Vanne Goodall was soon back to running the camp while her daughter began spending whole days, and nights too, out on the peak, where she set up a small auxiliary camp with a stove, coffeepot, and a metal trunk to hold a blanket and field notes.

She was still in the main camp one morning when an African arrived from the small village beyond the reserve. He urged both women to come with him to the little brick-and-mud hut where a young mother was lying, her newborn baby on the floor beside her. There were complications. The father had suggested bringing the Europeans to help. Unnerved, and not yet fluent enough in Swahili really to communicate, the Goodalls managed, nevertheless, to get an elderly African woman to help them. After a while both the new mother and her infant were fine.

Word spread. Soon Vanne Goodall was running a clinic at the lakeside camp. The childbirth was followed by an almost miraculous cure of an acute case of tropical ulcers—huge growths that had appeared on a patient's legs. Her reputation grew. The villagers feared the hospital in Kigoma, calling it a "place to die." So they flocked instead to Gombe, where Vanne Goodall gave out bandages and aspirin, and what advice she had learned from the first-aid books she had with her.

Through the clinic, the villagers got to know both women: the competent, extrovert mother, and the quiet, determined daughter. Besides fishing for the tiny dagaa, the villagers tilled small farms, cutting down the forest to plant cassavas and banana trees. The farmers had looked hungrily at the preserve, hoping the government would let them have the land to till. But after a while they accepted the permanence of the conservation scheme and many of them grew interested in Goodall's research.

Vanne Goodall, whose warmth won the confidence of these neighbors, was her eldest daughter's close friend. She made no demands on the younger woman, who pursued the elusive apes day after day. And when she would return to camp, excited one day, frustrated or depressed the next, Vanne Goodall listened sympathetically, discussing whatever the observations might imply.

She was waiting in camp the day her daughter made the first of her two astonishing discoveries, conveying news that ensured the continuation of the project. By this time Goodall had begun to recognize the chimpanzees individually, and she had given them names. She felt that these primates were much too special to be classified by number. So she named them, using a bit of whim. She called an old baldheaded male Mr. McGregor, after the crotchety farmer in Beatrix Potter's *Peter Rabbit;* and another David Graybeard, for the rim of white whiskers on his chin; and an unusually large male, Goliath, after the biblical giant. She became especially fond of an ugly female with ragged ears and a bulbous nose she named Flo. One day Flo, her sons Faben and Figan and Flint, and her daughter Fifi, would become central to Goodall's scientific studies.

It was David Graybeard who, in a way, made it all possible. A very intelligent animal, David was curious about this white primate and not really afraid of her. He allowed Goodall to watch him closely, from no farther than ten yards. It was autumn now, and the giant red termite hills that dot the region were full of life. In a few weeks the soldier termites would work their way up through the tunnels in their hills and fly off. Then the other animals would swoop down to try to snatch the juicy delicacies. But the chimpanzees, far more clever than the others, would get there first.

Goodall first noticed David Graybeard hard at work stripping a long stem of grass with his fingers and lips. She adjusted her binoculars and moved in closer. He was sitting next to a high red mound, a termite nest. As she watched, he pushed the stem into the mound and then withdrew it, covered with clinging insects. He licked them off as if he held a candy cane, then plunged the stem back into the nest.

She crouched for an hour, watching David. When he left, she rushed to the mound in time to see lines of worker termites mending the holes the chimpanzee had poked into their home. She decided to return to see if other chimps did the same thing, and she constructed a "hide," a shelter of palm leaves tied together at the top, where she could sit and wait without the chimps seeing her.

Seven days in a row she returned, but each time the chimps saw her and left. On the eighth day David reappeared with his friend Goliath, and the apes worked together for two hours, opening old holes in the mounds with their fingers. Goodall watched them carefully select blades of grass, and once she even saw Goliath wander fifteen feet away into the bush to select the perfect vine. This was the first time, as far as she knew, that anyone had seen a wild animal not only using a tool, but actually making one. She watched until she was convinced that this was not unusual; that, on the contrary, at Gombe the chimpanzees regularly termite, the mothers teaching the youngsters how to do it.

Excited, she telegraphed the news to Leakey in Nairobi. He replied by telegram: Either the definition of man must be changed (man was then described as a tool-using animal) or the chimpanzee had to be reclassified as human.

That same winter Goodall noticed a group of chimpanzees bustling around another chimpanzee who was eating something pink. The movements of a nearby female bush pig told the tale. The busy chimp was eating her baby, and the other excited apes were begging for a taste. Goodall watched for three hours until the feast was over. She had not witnessed the killing. But she realized that the chimpanzees obviously enjoyed eating meat. They were not, as primatologists had always supposed, vegetarians. In five months, Jane Goodall had learned more about the lives of wild chimpanzees than anyone had ever known before.

Once she wired this second piece of news to Leakey, he used it to generate publicity by broadcasting Goodall's remarkable discoveries to the world. Money was needed to continue financing the project and, headlines later, the National Geographic Society promised to continue funding the Gombe Project in return for the story as it unfolded.

The earliest primatologists had focused on ape anatomy. They knew that the chimpanzee is the smallest of the great apes and stands about five feet high and weighs somewhere between 125 and 175 pounds, with the females only slightly smaller than the males. They had found that although chimpanzees vary, all have brown skin and black, coarse, straight hair, which sometimes turns white around their chins, like David's beard. Chimps have large ears and small noses, brown eyes, and a bony ridge above their eyes. Some have another ridge, a sagittal crest, across the center of their heads that holds their large jaw muscles, making them look like they're wearing helmets. Their large mouths have big, mobile lips that they can twist into a smile or frown or pucker up for a kiss.

Primatologists were convinced that chimpanzees are vegetarians, although a few had been known to eat an egg occasionally, and all accepted meat in captivity. No one had supposed that chimps might like meat so much that they would hunt down large mammals to get it.

Earlier scientists also believed that chimpanzees moved mostly through the trees, swinging by their arms in a motion called brachiation. And although they knew that chimps could stand upright, they did not think that they did so very often. They had seen nests, but they believed that chimpanzees only made them once in a while, and then reused them, like campsites, when they found themselves near one at dusk.

Since Garner's time they knew that chimps make many different sounds with their throats, and also pound on the ground and on tree trunks. But they did not see any pattern to these noises and dismissed Garner's observations as a mixture of fantasy and wishful thinking, like his strange tale of the "carnival" he had claimed to witness in a rainstorm.

The scientists could not agree on the social structure of a chimpanzee community. Some primatologists believed the chimps moved about in family groups, like humans. But others thought that the groups were giant harems, and described the chimps in human social terms, calling them polygamous or promiscuous as well as egocentric, willful, and cowardly.

By the time Vanne Goodall returned to England in 1961, many of these old ideas had been revised by her daughter. She left the project financed for another year, and she left Jane Goodall to continue on her own.

Those first days alone were difficult. Vanne Goodall had been a buttress, a good friend as well as an excellent sounding board. But now Jane Goodall had begun habituating the wild animals. Patiently she let them get used to her presence so that they gradually accepted her as a natural part of their world. As habituated chimps, they acted normally around her and stopped running away at her approach. She became so involved in their lives that she forgot to be lonely.

For the next ten months solitude became her way of life. She felt her perceptions heighten. Trees, streams, and the very ground she trod acquired personalities. Colors grew more intense as she began to differentiate each subtle variation.

During these months she established a routine. Up at 5:30 A.M., she breakfasted on bread and coffee, then tucked a thermos and a can of meat into her knapsack. She always wore the same kind of dun-colored shorts, shirts, and tennis shoes so that she looked the same to the chimps. Then she tied her blond, shoulder-length hair into a ponytail and headed for the ripe fruit trees where she hoped to find the chimps. She tracked them from dawn to dusk, and sometimes slept precariously in the crotch of a tree, no nest cushioning her rest, so as not to miss anything the chimps might do.

Sometimes she found them still sleeping in their nests; sometimes she met them in their travels. She spent at least twelve hours of each day in the forest, but the amount of time she watched the chimps varied from a few minutes to many hours at a time. Occasionally she built a hide behind some fronds and branches. But she really wanted them to get used to her, so she only did this when she felt she had to see something very special, like the day she first watched David termiting. She realized they did not like to be watched, so if they noticed her, she pretended she was not at all interested in them, and concentrated on digging a hole, or even eating leaves, using their movements as a guide. She did not move away, for her goal was getting them used to having her around.

She wrote down everything she saw, not sifting anything, just getting it all down. Later, in the long evenings, she would sit outside and in the light of two hurricane lamps transpose her notes, sometimes filling up whole notebooks in just a day or so.

Five hundred yards away at first, then one hundred. After eight months the chimps let her come within fifty yards. After fourteen months, she could get within ten yards of them, and after eighteen months at Gombe, she was greeting David Graybeard and Goliath in her camp. By that time she had discovered that the large chimpanzee community at Gombe contained perhaps fifty animals which were constantly moving about from group to group. She began to note the patterns among them that persisted in spite of the changes. She sorted out some family groups, and even some family traits.

Goodall tasted everything that the chimpanzees ate, knowing that their systems are so similar to ours that their food could not harm her. Most of what they ate seemed sour, except for the weaver ants, which she found tasty, like curried lemons.

Later she would wash out their dung to get a clearer idea of how often they ate each food. Eating, she soon realized, took up at least seven of their waking hours. Most of their complex social behavior revolved around this activity. They squeezed the rest into the few remaining hours.

Then the October rains came, pushing the grass up as high as fourteen feet. Goodall had to climb the trees to track the chimpanzees, becoming as arboreal as they. She learned to take advantage of the torrents that washed away most of the trails and left the remaining few slippery and treacherous. The wet undergrowth silenced her footsteps, and the pounding rain drowned out the sound of her approach. Now she could come much closer to the chimpanzees, who sat all huddled into themselves, their hands around their knees, their heads hunched over. They seemed too miserable in the downpour to bother objecting to her.

The rainy season lasted longer than usual that year, and the temperature dropped to near freezing. She would wait, soaking on the slopes under a plastic sheet, watching the chimps in their sodden nests. These cold, wet mornings tried her dedication. It was hard to leave the warmth of her narrow camp bed, yet she did pull herself up, day after day, to follow the wet chimpanzees, that began to sneeze and sniffle as they caught colds in the miserable downpour.

One of those wintry days, as the rain came down, a clap of thunder startled her. At the same time it alerted the chimpanzees.

First one of the males stood erect and began swaying back and forth. He continued moving, building up momentum until suddenly he charged, running pell-mell down the slope until he caught onto the low branch of a tree and swung himself up. Immediately two more males dashed after him, breaking branches as they ran and tossing them into the air. The females and infants had escaped from the path of the males and were up in the branches of nearby trees, watching. Another male and still another took up the charge, pounding on the tree trunks as they went, and thumping on the ground. The performance lasted about twenty minutes, lit up erratically by streaks of lightning. So this was the "carnival" that Richard Garner had described— a challenge to the elements, an act of defiance!

The rains passed in the early spring and another dry season gave Goodall more time to habituate the chimpanzees. By the time the rains returned in late 1961, Louis Leakey, who had decided it was time for his young protégé to get the proper academic credentials, had arranged for her to study animal behavior. Cambridge University had agreed to waive her lack of undergraduate training. Leakey realized that she had made enormous strides on her own, but she had to learn professional techniques in order to go further and win the respect of the academic world.

That first term at Cambridge passed painfully for the young scientist. She felt exiled from Gombe, where David, Goliath, and the Flo family lived their days without her. That spring, leaving Cambridge, Goodall began to cast off both her shyness and the diffidence of the amateur. She stepped onto the lecture podium for the first time in London, explaining with great precision, and charm, what she had observed among the chimps.

When she returned to Gombe in the summer of 1962, she brought with her new confidence, new methods, and a typewriter. Her African staff welcomed her back, and so in a way did David Graybeard. For soon after her return an oil-nut palm tree above her tent came into fruit and, when she returned to camp one evening, her staff told her that while she had been gone, David had come to camp to dine.

Feasting on palm nuts one day, David Graybeard, both

curious and bold, snatched some bananas from Goodall's work-table. Thus began a new phase of life at Gombe. Soon Goodall was sending uplake to Mwamgongo, the nearest village, for huge supplies of bananas. Within a few weeks David brought his friend Goliath into camp to share the delicacy. Soon there were a dozen wild chimpanzees, the same creatures she had searched for so desperately two years earlier, raiding her campsite for this special food.

They developed a taste for raw eggs too, and discovered that humans' towels and tee shirts get saturated with the salt of sweat, which made them good for sucking. They also discovered that the canvas of the tents made excellent chewing.

Ugly old Flo was one of the chimps who followed David and Goliath into camp. When she was in estrus, despite her ragged ears and bulbous nose, the male chimps were eager to mate with her. Female chimps have a monthly cycle during which the sex skin at their rumps gradually expands and becomes very pink, and then recedes again. When this "flowering" is most apparent, the female is in estrus and ready to conceive. All females in estrus attract male chimps, but Flo was unusually popular. With Flo came her then adolescent sons, Figan and Faben, and her small daughter, Fifi. Goodall began to play with these small animals, wrestling with Figan and tickling him. But when she realized that she had stepped over the line from habituating them into taming them, she stopped. She was also endangering both herself and other future human observers. Adult chimpanzees are much stronger than humans. And while the infants enjoyed playing, all in good fun, the same animal, full grown, could initiate the same games and accidentally squeeze the life out of its human playmate.

That summer the National Geographic Society decided to send a professional photographer to record the startling observations Goodall was reporting from Gombe. At Leakey's suggestion, they sent Baron Hugo Van Lawick, a Dutch animal lover who had been making films of African wildlife in Kenya. The day after his arrival, David Graybeard came to camp, peeped into his tent, and more or less introduced himself. The other chimpanzees accepted this new human as readily as they now accepted the female of the species—Jane Goodall.

After Van Lawick left, Goodall remained at Gombe until she had to return to Cambridge for another term. Meanwhile her *National Geographic* articles proved so popular that they decided to send the photographer back the following summer to get more pictures. This time when Van Lawick and Goodall parted, just before Christmas in 1963, he sent a telegram to her the next day.

Van Lawick suggested that they get married. And as soon as she completed the next term at the university, they did. The wedding took place in London, in the summer of 1964. But they returned to Gombe almost immediately afterward. Flo had given birth to a son, whom Goodall dubbed Flint. He was the first chimp whose life she was able to document from the beginning.

Within a few years the shy Englishwoman had become a celebrity. Van Lawick's films for the National Geographic Society and her autobiographical books, combined with her success on the lecture circuit, pushed her into prominence. In 1967 Hugo Van Lawick, Jr., nicknamed Grub, was born. Goodall began spending more and more time away from Gombe—lecturing, directing students (for she was a professor now), and investigating other African wildlife with her husband and child. Yet she continued spending part of each year at Gombe, supervising the chimpanzee research. Her work, and the remarkable photographic records of Van Lawick, made an accurate picture of chimp behavior more widely available than ever before.

2

A Day of Tracking

Morning

Dawn slips over the eastern mountains and the sun's slanted rays reach into the green world of the *miombo* tree. Fifi and her son, Freud, are asleep there together, and Fifi's old mother, Flo, is resting nearby with Flint, who is now eight years old. The human observers, perched in the branches of another tree, have been listening to the forest's nighttime voices and trying not to slip down for almost an hour. They rejoice silently as the chimps finally wake up, stretch, and yawn.

Twelve hours earlier they had watched Fifi build her nest eighty feet above the ground. Selecting a nice forked tree limb, she had bent some smaller branches toward herself, holding them down with her feet. Then she crisscrossed them into place. While she broke off small twigs and leaves to cushion the bed, little Freud had been watching. When she was done, he had climbed in beside her. The whole process had taken five minutes.

Freud is like all the other wild-born chimpanzees in Africa, yet he is distinct because he is one of a community of thirty animals at Gombe whose lives have been carefully observed by humans for fifteen years. Jane Goodall had watched his grandmother Flo raise Fifi. Now Goodall and her students are curiously watching how Fifi raises her own child.

Astride the sturdy branches, field glasses to their eyes, the observers can see Fifi gently tumbling little Freud with her feet as she lies in her nest. Then she starts to tickle him and after a while they both sit up and she "grooms" his soft brown hair. Her dark fingers comb through, parting Freud's hair down to his light skin. She tosses away flecks of dry skin and leaves. Occasionally she finds tiny seeds he picked up in his travels and pops them into her mouth. Chimpanzees do not harbor parasites in their hair, for they are nomads and do not stay in one place long enough for fleas or lice to hatch. Now she is grooming Freud with her mouth, a gesture that leads some behavioral biologists to suggest that grooming in primates is the evolutionary ancestor of caressing between human beings. It is clear to the observers that the animals enjoy being groomed.

Freud's bottom sports white hairs that he will lose gradually as he grows up. She grooms these too, before he swings onto her back. At three years of age, Freud rides along on top of her in what Goodall calls "jockey-fashion" because the small chimp looks like a rider atop a racehorse.

Fifi swings down from the miombo tree to the forest floor with Freud holding on tight atop her. Sometimes she may swing from tree to tree, but like most adult chimpanzees, Fifi usually travels along the ground. She moves on all fours, leaning on the thick layers of cartilage that protect the backs of her hands from the rough earth. These knuckle pads are a peculiar adaptation that have evolved to help protect the chimps' sensitive hands.

Through the forest and into a meadow where the savanna grasses rise to at least five feet, both Fifi and Flo, who has been following her, now pause. They take their bearings, standing upright in order to see above the grass until they spot what they are after. Down on all fours again, they hurry ahead. Freud clings to his mother's long back hairs, but Flint moves along independently at Flo's heels. They do not stop until they reach the large red termite mound.

Then the observers stop too, about fifteen feet away from the chimps, and sit down with legs akimbo, pushing down the vines and tall grasses that block their view. Although the chimps are aware of the humans, the observers try to remain inconspicuous. They know that their presence makes the animals uneasy.

They follow Fifi's movements carefully as she feels the mound with her sensitive fingertips and then unplugs the opening to one of the passageways. Fifi learned to fish for termites by watching her own mother, Flo. Now Freud is acquiring the same skill by watching Fifi choose a long piece of grass just as David Gray-beard did, and pare it down until it is slim enough to fit into the opening. Fifi thrusts it in and pulls it out again, all covered with clinging termites. As she licks them off greedily, Freud decides to try it too. He looks around for a tool, picks a flimsy piece of grass, and jabs it at the mound, with no success. By the time he is five he should be an expert. At the moment, however, he is becoming an increasingly frustrated young animal.

Flo is totally absorbed in termiting, an occupation that the females seem to prefer. But Flint, who has fished a little, is tired of the sport and does not bother with the mound. Flint is old enough to be spending most of his time with other juveniles. Yet he is so attached to Flo that he hangs around, tugging at her intermittently. He is obviously bored and anxious to move on.

Small chimpanzees vary almost as much as human children. How rapidly a child becomes independent depends on its own temperament, its mother's attitude, and where it happened to arrive in order of birth. First children sometimes suffer from amateur mothers, and some first-born chimpanzees actually die from her innocent neglect. But those that survive may thrive in the uniqueness that no other offspring after them enjoys. Among the chimpanzees we can also see how the arrival of the next baby —usually when the first chimp is about five, but never sooner— forces the juvenile out of the nest and into a new stage of life.

Youngsters like Freud depend on their mothers for comfort and guidance more than any other primate except humans. One of the most important of Goodall's revelations has been how really long these years of dependency are. Little Freud clung to his mother's stomach, drinking her milk when he was hungry, for six months. He was in contact with her all the time except for brief occasions when she "hung him up" on a low branch so she could reach for something special to eat. By the time Freud had his first birthday, he had begun to eat solid foods and had learned to ride on Fifi's back.

At three, he is still nursing and should continue seeking her nipple until Fifi is pregnant once again. Even then she will not push him away until her milk dries up. Mother chimps seem to understand that their youngsters need the comfort of suckling as much as they need the milk. And during this time, Freud shares Fifi's nest. Later on, when another baby may demand her total care, Fifi would still offer Freud her protection, just as her mother, Flo, still comes to the aid of Fifi's older brothers, Figan and Faben.

But right now Freud is still trying to termite and he has given up fishing for his own and is begging Fifi for some of hers, his small hand out, palm upward in the same gesture that humans make. But Fifi is too busy to respond to him. Freud, in his anger, begins to scream. At the same time he crouches low and clutches his stomach as if he has cramps and puckers his lips in a pout. As Freud screeches, Fifi keeps eating. The observers wonder how long she can go on ignoring this tantrum. Freud's fury unabated, he rolls over on the ground, grabs some dry grass, and tosses it. In a final effort, he runs over to Fifi and begins pounding on her with his small hands.

Fifi finally gives in and lets him lick a stemful of termites. Freud's screams fade to a whimper and then stop altogether.

Fifi has been giving in to Freud's temper tantrums since he first had them when he was just a few weeks old. When she left him for a few minutes then, he started this same kind of intense, irrational screaming. As Freud grew older, he performed in this way whenever he happened to lose sight or feel of Fifi, even for a short time. Now he is raging because he cannot share her special food. Experience has taught him that tantrums win concessions. Calmed down now, he is smacking his lips, still fresh with the juice of termites.

Freud is just entering that stage of life that Goodall says should last another five years. As a juvenile, Freud will begin to play with other small chimpanzees and will absorb the subtle rules of life among the members of the Gombe community.

Flint is at the far end of this juvenile stage, and is really on the brink of the next stage—adolescence. Too big to ride astride Flo anymore, he moves restlessly around the clearing. It is as hard for young apes to grow up as it is for people. And it seems to be much more difficult for the males than for the females in the chimp society.

Fifi began to menstruate sometime between her seventh and tenth years. At about the same time she began showing a pink "flower" at her rump once a month. But for the first year that she showed the swelling, it was not as large as it eventually became when she was fully mature. During that year she seldom mated, and when she did, it was usually with adolescent males. At about the age of nine she showed her first fully adult swelling and attracted adult male chimps. When she was about eleven, Freud was born, and Fifi did not go into estrus again during the next three years. Fifi will resume estrus cycles sometime during Freud's fourth year and, although she may become pregnant, she will still nurse Freud.

Young males suffer a longer adolescence. At about eight years of age they begin a tremendous growth spurt and at about the same time they begin to put on more frequent violent displays. Flo's older sons, Figan and Faben, had to make a place for themselves within the larger community. Suddenly Flo's protection was not enough. They used these displays to maneuver with older males—as well as with male peers—for a place in the hierarchy. Most males Flint's age already spend more of their time with "the boys." But Flint is Flo's last child, and she lets him stay with her. Flint feels secure with Fifi too, who as a juvenile used to try to mother him. Once in a while Flint does follow Figan and Faben. But usually he is content to be with the females.

The observers look at their watches. An hour has passed since Fifi and Flo started termiting. The humans are getting cramped and are relieved when Flint manages to distract Flo permanently. The small family moves across the meadow and heads for a ripe fig tree on a nearby slope.

The observers follow, keeping at least five yards' distance. They stop quickly when they see Flo, and then Fifi, halt, their body hair on end, making them look much bigger than they really are. The observers hold their breath; they cannot see what has frightened the chimps.

But they can hear it. Branches crashing much too close, with no place to hide. The noise rises to a deafening pitch as the chimps bark and screech in fright. Flo's mouth drops open in a full grin, exposing all her teeth, the usual expression of a terrified chimp. Within seconds a herd of wild buffalo rush past the chimps and then veer off in another direction. They are used to chimps, but they probably caught the scent of humans, which enraged them. As the buffalo move on, Fifi and Flo let their hair fall back in place. But the chimps, in their fear, exuded a pungent smell that lingers where they halted. Now the humans inhale it as they pass by, hurrying to catch up with the animals at the fig trees.

Figan and Faben and half a dozen other chimpanzees at the fig tree greet the newcomers. They screech excitedly at each other and Figan puts his great arms around Fifi and pats Freud on the head. After the females have been recognized and accepted, they all return to eating, silently. Figan's mouth is open but his lips cover his teeth in a relaxed expression, a "play-face." Once in a while he utters a low, panting *hoo waa,* and then responding grunts of *ugh-e-ugh* seem to indicate that the fruit is good and plentiful. Flo and Fifi echo these sounds as they begin eating seriously. They pucker their lips to sound the *hoo* and open up wide to make the *waa.* Goodall has isolated twenty-three different vocalizations that the chimps make when playing together, threatening other animals, discovering a new food supply, or simply greeting each other.

The chimps respond quickly to all changes, going into a flurry of noisy excitement whenever a new individual joins them. They bark sharply, and from a distance sound like dogs. But they calm down again just as rapidly. Enjoying the sweet figs, Flo barks between bites, letting her jaw hang open with her bottom teeth showing. The chimps feed a long time on the fruit, until the sun is directly overhead in the wide African sky. Then, full for a while, at least, they climb down from the tree and look for a shady spot of grass. Here they sprawl out for their noontime nap.

During the rainy season the chimps build day nests in the trees for their siestas. But on a nice dry day like this one, they are quite comfortable on the spongy, grass-covered ground. Arms and legs akimbo, the adults stretch out to sleep—but not the youngsters.

Freud likes to play with things that he finds in the world around him. He discovers a round fruit the size of a tennis ball that he rolls down the slope, then rushes to catch it and hurries back. Although Fifi is asleep, Freud stays close to her. His "soccer" practice with his "ball" reminds the observers of the way his mother liked to play when she was small. Young Fifi once pulled a dead rat around by its tail, making it into a pull-toy.

Freud now spots his uncle Flint and starts to chase him. Flint looks over his shoulder, sure that Freud is still there, and leads him a merry zigzag lark up through the branches of a nearby tree. Still light, both young animals use their long arms to brachiate. Back on the ground again, Flint lets Freud catch up with him.

Then over and over they go together, wrestling and tumbling, picking up dried grass and leaves in their hair as they roll. The observers time this rough-and-tumble play: twenty minutes, and the only sound they hear is a soft, panting gasp, the chimp equivalent of laughter. Through their field glasses they can see Freud's face most of the time. He keeps his mouth ajar, with his lips pulled back, showing his baby teeth in a smile.

They roll apart and Flint seems ready for a rest. But Freud is still full of energy, so he races away and climbs right up on top of his full-grown uncle, Figan. The humans look at each other fearfully. Figan is asleep and does not like rude awakenings. But they relax as they see this huge male animal only lightly cuff the infant, then turn over and go back to sleep.

Chastised, Freud scurries back to Fifi and seeks her breast. He stays close to her now. The other grown chimpanzees, sprawled all over the sun-dappled clearing, are waking up.

Faben moves over toward Figan and sits down beside him. With his head bent forward, he examines his brother's hair. Carefully, he parts it with his fingernail, just as Fifi combed Freud at daybreak.

Grooming is probably the most important social activity among chimps. Of course they keep clean this way, but they could easily groom themselves. Instead, they have turned grooming into a way of expressing mutual concern with physical contact. When the brothers are apart for a few days, they greet each other with loud screeches, then set to grooming each other.

Now Flint has finally left Flo's immediate presence. He moves cautiously toward a large adult male. Uneasy, body hair erect, Flint crouches low before the imposing animal and starts to groom him. The adult male allows himself to be groomed. In return, he pats Flint's head and grooms him for a few moments. The observers can actually see Flint relax; his erect hairs fall back as he steps back and sits in the aura of this leader.

The group today is rather large. Half a dozen females with their children, and many adolescent and adult males are lolling in the sunlight, or grooming each other. One large female, Gigi, is full grown and seems to be sterile. She has never been seen with an infant, not even a dead baby, as had been the case with several other adult females. Gigi goes on patrol with the adult males when they "police" the borders of their territory. She is romping with the males now, and usually plays the tomboy role. Yet when she is in estrus, she is extremely popular sexually. Between these times, however, she is "one of the boys," a curious pattern that is still not understood.

The observers recognize and have named each member of this chimpanzee community. So they notice when a stranger, a new female, suddenly saunters into the group. Her pink rump announces that she is in estrus, which the observers know may last ten days, or even longer. Old Flo once stayed that way for five weeks.

Flirtatiously, this newcomer presents herself, bending down and thrusting her rump toward the crowd of interested males. The adolescent males come up to examine her while the adult females ignore her altogether. Should Fifi come into estrus now, most likely Freud would try to fight off all her suitors. But only a female's own children are disturbed by mating. The others take it in their stride, watching with interest as one by one, almost as if they are taking turns, the males approach this visiting female from the rear and mate with her.

Female chimpanzees appear as if they will mate with any male who wants to and do not care the least about which one it is. But closer observations reveal that this is only half the story. The female's time in estrus is quite long. She is only accessible to every male at the beginning. But when she is most fertile, many females leave the group for a few days with one special male. Ethologists call this "safari" behavior, for the pair are off on a kind of African honeymoon. Most probably this safari partner will be the one to father the infant, should she become pregnant. Primatologists are curious to learn if the female will go off on safari with the same male month after month. This seems likely. A bigger question is, Will she choose the same male five years later, when she is ready to have another baby?

Meanwhile the observers note down that a strange female has apparently joined the community. It is common for females in estrus to move on from one group to another. Should this new female have a baby, they will both probably stay with this group. It is probably a way of spreading the gene pool and assuring that the chimpanzee communities do not become inbred. The practice reminds Goodall of certain human cultures that routinely send their daughters off to live far from home with her bridegroom's family.

After a while the new female wanders off into the trees with one adult male. Now that her exciting presence is gone, the large gathering begins to break up.

Afternoon

The day wears on, lazily. The sun casts longer shadows in the clearing, and some of the chimps that lay down in the shade are now highlighted. All have begun to move. Many have already wandered off.

The observers watch the gathering break into smaller groups. They let the females go and wait to track Figan. Musing in the quiet lull, they remember other chimpanzees who used to live at Gombe. In the wild, lucky chimps live to be about thirty years old, but that is only a guess. In captivity, chimps can live another fifteen years with the help of good food, medicine, and doctoring. Unlucky chimps succumb to illness and accidents. When a polio epidemic swept Gombe in 1967, Goodall saw six familiar faces pass away. Other individuals recovered, like Faben, with a paralyzed right arm. Chimps suffer all the viral diseases that plague humans, especially lung infections such as pneumonia.

Other animals have died in fights, particularly in January, when the popular milk-apple tree is ripe. Then chimpanzees from more than one community compete for the prized food.

Although chimps are very sociable and move about with ever-changing sets of friends, the animals that roam the thirty-square-mile range fall into a definite hierarchy. They may travel in groups as large as six, or a male may travel alone. Today's companions may not meet for weeks. But when they reunite, they all understand their place within the group.

Ethologists call the top male the Alpha animal. To hold his leadership, he must constantly show his power. Over the years, Goodall has seen the Alpha spot passed on from animal to animal. David's friend Goliath held the position when Goodall first arrived. He managed to confound his subordinates by performing a one-man show of strength, featuring a lot of running about and tossing or dragging huge, leafy branches that he broke off to emphasize his prowess.

But he was eventually displaced by a very low-ranking male who was clever enough to take advantage of the empty kerosene cans that the humans left around their campsite. He learned somehow to line up several of these four-gallon cans and hit or kick them clangingly as he performed his own "display," a tremendous outpouring of noise and motion, an adult tantrum, that males put on to impress an audience of other males, females, and sometimes even human beings. This ape held the top position for six years. Even after Goodall removed the cans, he incorporated other man-made objects into his act, such as chairs or pieces of roofing material.

But as this Alpha male also aged, the other animals gradually stopped watching his performances. One day a young and very powerful male displaced him. But he, in turn, gave way to a new phenomenon, the brothers Figan and Faben, who actually cooperated in replacing the leader and taking dual command.

Each Alpha male achieved power differently. The first was strong and aggressive, the next technically ingenious. The third was overwhelmingly large and powerful, and the last two were skilled in cooperating.

The observers are following Figan now, and are not at all surprised to see him brush up against another male that left the gathering earlier. The lesser animal backs away submissively to let Figan pass. Within the group each animal knows his position in relation to the others. They usually avoid fighting because the lower animal acknowledges the other's superiority by moving away, just as this male has done. If Figan had been more forceful, the other male would have bowed submissively to him, or started grooming him.

But when dominant males from different communities meet, battles may rage. The strangers bite and scratch each other and occasionally use a branch as a weapon, injuring one another seriously. Real fighting within a group is rare, though brief fights are common. But any animal becomes a stranger if it has not been in touch with the group for only a day and is not related to the immediate animals in the group. They seem instinctively to fear strangers. The Gombe team began to notice more violence as they became familiar with the borders of the territory of the habituated animals. They observed the male chimps taking turns patrolling these borders. When the patrol found nests built by stranger chimps, they tore them apart viciously.

At first it seemed that the chimps only attacked strangers that invaded their territory. Later, trackers watched Figan and Faben actually move into the territory of another group and attack weak adult chimps and kill infants.

It may be that the cultivation of land outside the Gombe Stream Reserve has forced other wild chimpanzees into the park, crowding the apes and provoking more aggression. It may be that they have always been aggressive but that such behavior was not observed until recently. This disturbing discovery of unprovoked aggression is one aspect of chimp behavior that Goodall is especially interested in exploring further.

But within the community, the chimps funnel tension into safer channels. The common way seems to be the kind of display that Goodall witnessed first during her lonely rainy season at Gombe. Then the animals were challenging the elements. In more day-to-day drama, the Alpha male puts on a display to affirm his position. Periodically a rival for power may compete with him, breaking off branches, stamping the ground, leaping into the air, and occasionally hurling rocks, as David Graybeard once did when Hugo Van Lawick arrived at Gombe. That day David heaved a rock right through the tent, missing Van Lawick by only two inches.

But no one is fighting now. Figan has passed the other male and is continuing along, leaning on his knuckle pads. He goes deeper into the gallery forest, where leafy trees scarcely allow any sunlight to work its way down to the soft earth. Suddenly he stops. The hairs on his body rise up. He looks around and scratches himself vigorously. The observers look for what is bothering him and realize that it is themselves. They have come too close, and Figan does not like being watched. They move back and away, behind a broad tree trunk.

A thrashing of branches stops Figan's movements; the observers hesitate too. The noise is coming from way over their heads. They stand back, field glasses to their eyes, and scan the trees. Far up on a high branch they see an adolescent chimp, not much larger than Flint, in fact, holding onto a red colobus monkey with his teeth. It looks as if he found the small victim by chance and killed him on the spot. Now he is tearing at the pink flesh and suddenly Figan is up there beside him and Faben, his paralyzed arm hanging at his side, has also appeared. Both are begging for a taste.

The proprietor of the small kill is very young. And although he ranks very low within the community, the Alpha males, Figan and Faben, do not take it from him. But they do hang around, screeching and embracing each other in excited staccato motions. Another adult male arrives, and so do several females, all anxious for a piece of meat.

Figan and Faben receive a handout, but the hunter keeps the rest for himself and does not give it to later arrivals. The ignored hungry male watches the others eating, obviously enraged. His face is set in a full-closed grin, teeth clenched together, lips open, absorbing the humiliation. His hair rises on end now, and he raises his arm to strike a blow. But he does not strike Figan and Faben, the Alpha males; instead he reaches out and cuffs one of the females. He redirects his frustration: it is a common way for chimps to blow off steam without getting into a fight. It is just as common among human beings, when, for instance, a teacher may correct a student, who in turn takes it out on someone else, perhaps a younger sibling at home.

The small monkey's body disappears as the observers watch. The best part, the brain, is left to the young hunter to enjoy. He pulls a few leaves off a branch, then he carefully bunches the leaves together, and uses them to sop up the soft brains from the skull cavity. He has quickly used something close at hand as a tool to make eating easier.

The other chimpanzees move on now, but their mood has changed. Figan and Faben stay together, and the other animals who joined in the feast do not stray far. Following ten yards behind, the observers sense something else about to happen.

Then it does. A young baboon has lagged more than two hundred yards behind the large baboon troop. Feeding in a fig tree, he probably did not notice that he had been left behind. One of the younger chimps climbs into the same tree, a couple of feet higher than the baboon. On the ground, Figan signals Faben and three other chimpanzees, who move, stationing themselves near the base of the fig and three other trees. They have blocked the baboon's escape routes.

The victim spots the chimpanzees lurking below him. He utters a high-pitched baboon bark, and leaps into another tree. But the chimps move along with him. The taste of meat fresh on their lips, they crave more. They seem to be coordinating their attack. Up in the branches of this new tree, the same young male chimp waits poised above the young baboon.

The terrified baboon screams again. Below him, chimpanzees block every exit. He backs up, right into the clutches of the young hunter.

The prospect of a feast has stimulated a circus of screams. As always, when they are moved emotionally, they seek physical contact with each other. Now they are clutching and embracing one another with frenzied gestures.

This hunt was viewed as a cooperative action. Different animals took different positions, and they did not fight over which one actually made the kill. The observers know that they had to communicate with each other to do this, but they are not at all sure how the chimps organized their attack, and how much might have been prearranged.

Meanwhile, the loud *hoos* and barks have attracted more chimpanzees, including Fifi and Freud. All of them defer to the young male who actually made the kill, and let him choose the choice tidbits. But they cluster around as the hunter moves down to the ground with his kill. It is large enough to feed the entire group.

The newcomers beg, noisily. The hunter tears off pieces of the carcass with his teeth and gives it to members of the crowd, including the low-ranking male who was left out of the smaller kill.

As they eat, the chimpanzees pull handfuls of leaves, which they swallow along with the meat. Fifi chews a wad of leaves and meat and then spits it into Freud's small hand. More unusual, Figan chews some meat the same way and spits it into the hand of a nearby animal. This is the only occasion when nonhuman primates, except for mothers and babies, have been seen sharing food.

The observers count the "guests" at the feast. Fifteen chimpanzees in all, and although they did not get equal portions, they all got something. Figan and Faben, the Alpha animals, and the visiting female in estrus got the largest shares after the hunter himself. But all the animals seem content.

Sated, they move off, taking separate paths through the trees. The observers continue tracking Figan and Faben, who stop together beside a fallen tree. The thirsty chimps see water in a narrow hole in the log, too small to get their snouts into. The chimps find some leaves and chew them lightly. They have made the leaves into sponges, which they dip into the water and then suck.

The chimps move faster now, and the observers have to run to keep up. But the animals stop short when they reach a stream. The observers know that the chimps hate to wet their feet and wonder what they will do. Figan grabs an overhanging branch and brachiates, swinging over the obstacle to a tree across the water. But Fagen, with his useless arm, cannot swing easily. Instead, he finds stones to step on and, carefully upright, he walks across. The humans follow quickly, wading through the cool, clean water.

Although the animals are quite stuffed from their feast, they stop occasionally as they move on, picking berries with their fingers from a low bush and stuffing them into their mouths. They are eating lackadaisically, as much out of habit, it appears, as out of hunger.

Figan gazes up through the leafy canopy toward the sky. The observers follow his gaze. The sun looks as if it is about to plummet into Lake Tanganyika. They peer at their watches. Almost six o'clock. Figan too knows the day is ending and he finds a broad miombo tree like the one his sister, Fifi, slept in the night before. But he chooses a sturdy branch less than fifteen feet from the ground to build his nest. Cicadas shrill into the dusk, and the night birds begin a piping chant. Somewhere a chimpanzee *hoos* and Figan answers.

Figan surveys his new nest, hesitates, then reaches out for a last leafy branch. He cracks it off and tucks this final cushion into a pillow beneath his head. As he curls up to sleep, the night begins to blur the thick foliage, obscuring him from the observers' view. They note down the time and place, then turn quietly away and head back toward camp.

3

A Bigger Gombe

Jane Goodall returned to Gombe immediately after her marriage to Hugo Van Lawick in 1964. She surveyed the research, almost completed for her doctoral dissertation, and saw it from a new perspective as only the first stage of what she envisioned as a long-range project. She realized that she could use the help of the volunteers who had begun to write, asking if they could become part of the scientific adventure at Gombe.

The first to reach Africa, a young woman from Peru, was followed within months by a second in 1965. These early volunteers were enthusiastic but untrained, and helped Goodall mostly by relieving her of a lot of paper work. Later, in 1970, trained students arrived from Cambridge University and from Stanford University to study the animals and help keep the increasingly detailed records she was gathering on the chimpanzees, and eventually on the lives of baboons and red colobus monkeys as well.

The Tanzanian government incorporated the old chimpanzee reserve into its larger national park system in 1968. At almost the same time, Dr. Goodall was appointed director of the scientific field station that had been renamed the Gombe Stream Research Center. The Center began to develop ties with universities on three continents: to Cambridge in England, where Goodall had received her Ph.D. in 1965; Stanford in California, where she was a visiting professor from 1971 to 1975; and the university at Dar es Salaam, on the other side of Tanzania. The 1970s saw an intensification of research as Gombe became allied with the new Serengeti Research Institute, which is concerned with research in all of Tanzania's national parks.

Meanwhile, the chimpanzees had also changed. Once they had lost their fear of humans, they made themselves too much at home. Apes invaded everything. They upset personal belongings and scattered the patiently accumulated scientific data everywhere. Tent living had lost its magic. So Goodall was delighted in 1965 when the National Geographic Society, which had continued sponsoring her work, gave her the money to begin constructing what would eventually become more than a dozen simple buildings at Gombe.

There are no roads into the wilderness around the lakefront, so everything had to be done by hand. Van Lawick and the African staff carried the relatively lightweight, but still cumbersome, prefabricated aluminum sidings up the narrow trail several miles from the beach to a place where the view was glorious and the chimpanzees close. Then they had to clear a level site on the slope for the cement foundation. When a rock proved too stubborn, they just left it jutting up through the rough slab floor.

Finally the first two huts were finished, their roofs grassed over to insulate them from the heat and, almost as important to Goodall, to help them blend in harmoniously with the lush landscape. Van Lawick helped clear an area about the size of a football field where they could observe and photograph the chimpanzees without foliage.

Her next project was moving the banana boxes away from the huts to an area that would keep the chimpanzees visiting, but not visiting at home. The situation had grown complicated because the noisy, gregarious baboons had also discovered the bananas and were just as fond of the treat as the chimps. She had to do something that would put her back in control of the situation.

She liked the idea of a "feeding station." It was an excellent way to get to know the individuals and to watch them as they interacted in a group. David, of course, had brought his friend Goliath into the camp, and soon the Flo family came too. As Flo became habituated, accepting Goodall as just another animal, she allowed the human to approach and even touch her new infant, who in 1965 was Flint. Goodall believes that she got to know the wild animals better in a shorter span of time by feeding them bananas than she ever could have done by observing them among the trees. An artificial feeding station seemed an ideal way of keeping the chimps close while regaining some of her lost privacy.

But the bananas began to attract more and more chimps. And as the crowd grew, their behavior changed. Fifty chimpanzees at a time began showing up at the site, and soon equal numbers of hungry baboons came. The animals began fighting among themselves, and between the species, all greedy for the delicacy. The introduction of a seemingly endless supply of an especially popular food had changed the community. After three years, the chimps had learned to hurl rocks at the baboons and at each other. They were living in what could almost be described as a state of war, and human interference was responsible.

Something had to be done. She could, of course, have shut down the feeding station altogether. The animals would have accepted this. They were, after all, used to trees heavy with fruit suddenly barren for years at a time. But Goodall did not want to give up the chimps' regular visits.

Eventually, after much trial and many errors, she and Hugo Van Lawick devised a system of about thirty concrete bunkers which were sunk into the earth at scattered intervals. Each bunker had two doors, the visible one up front that the chimps could open easily but the less clever baboons could not, and a door concealed in the rear for humans only. The bunker was divided by a false wall that allowed Goodall to keep a supply of bananas hidden in the rear compartment. She could raise the false wall by pulling a handle ten yards away, thus tumbling bananas into the front section when she wanted to feed a particular chimpanzee.

A chimpanzee asleep in the nest it has made.
Below, males brachiating during a charging display.

From *In the Shadow of Man* (1971)
by Jane Van Lawick-Goodall

From *In the Shadow of Man* (1971)
by Jane Van Lawick-Goodall

Flo grooming her juvenile son, Flint.
After they have stripped leaves from twigs to use as tools, these chimpanzees are ready to fish termites out of the mound.

Jane Goodall, National Geographic Society

A quiet moment at the Gombe Stream camp as Jane Goodall and a chimp exchange affection.

Stanford Outdoor Primate Facility

Chimpanzee play area at the Stanford Outdoor Primate Facility. The cement boxes in the foreground rest on wooden posts, providing shelter for the chimps. Inset, above left, a thirteen-year-old female with her infant daughter, members of the chimpanzee community at Stanford.

Goodall eventually arrived at a system that kept track of which chimpanzee had eaten bananas at what time. Then each animal got fed only once every two or three weeks. When a chimp wandered into chimp camp, it checked out the banana boxes. But the odds were against its finding food there, so the animals did not bother traveling to the camp if they were far off in other parts of the park.

When the feeding station stopped being a cornucopia for the chimps, the state of war faded into a gentle truce. But a curious thing gradually happened. The chimpanzees that had been meeting and even sleeping in nests around the feeding station split into two groups, the northern group, the Kikombe community, and the southern group, the Kahama community. Goodall does not know if there actually had been two chimpanzee communities before she set up the feeding station, or if the tense atmosphere that developed in the competition for bananas triggered the split. Whatever the situation was before, her 1974 studies prove that two quite distinct communities exist at Gombe now, each with its own top-ranking Alpha male and a whole constellation of lower-ranking animals. These groups are hostile to each other and the northern group seems determined to eliminate or absorb the southern group. When the animals separated, Goliath went south while Figan and Faben stayed in the north. When the milk-apple tree deep inside the southern territory came into bloom, the northern animals traveled down for their favorite treat. They apparently heard the calls of Goliath and his friends and set out to find and attack him. They set upon him brutally; five former comrades, including Figan and Faben, beat him steadily for twenty minutes, obviously trying to kill him. They left him so battered that he did die soon after, a victim of their assault.

Some primate ethologists question the whole banana-feeding scheme. They argue that in giving the chimpanzees a food that they could not naturally find at Gombe, Goodall intervened with their "natural" environment. They suggest that Goodall literally took the "wild" out of the Gombe chimps, that she created an artificially large chimpanzee group that has now returned to normal. Conceding that she did make some errors as she groped to establish new rules for this kind of ethological research, she does not include the feeding station as one of them.

She admits she should never have touched the wild animals who allowed her to groom them, like David Graybeard and the baby Flint. There is potential physical danger, and there is the scientific danger of changing the animal's behavior. There is also the psychological danger of becoming emotionally involved with the individual animals. Such involvement could bias scientific judgment.

Chimp camp, the feeding station, was just the beginning of

new building sites at Gombe. Soon Goodall abandoned some of her earlier camps, like the Peak where she had slept alone with her metal trunk and coffeepot during her first year there. For a while, in the mid-1960s, when there were still only a handful of people, she kept a "haystack on stilts," a picturesque three-sided wilderness kitchen that they used when they were out tracking in the bush.

But soon Gombe outgrew this too. More people had arrived to study baboons under Goodall's direction, and they set up headquarters on the lakeshore near the African village. In 1974 her personal life changed when she and Hugo Van Lawick were divorced. Subsequently she married Derek Bryceson, director of Tanzania's national parks. By May 1975, the Gombe Stream Research Center had grown to include about eight graduate students, ten Stanford undergraduates, and ten permanent Tanzanian trackers who had been especially trained in animal observation. She had a mess hall built and hired three cooks to feed the crew. Altogether there was a Tanzanian community amounting to fifty people.

By this time Jane Goodall was living in a two-bedroom house which she shared with her small son and his English tutor when she was not with Derek Bryceson at their home in Dar es Salaam. The rest of the students and scientists shared small, prefabricated-metal huts that were scattered unobtrusively against the slopes near chimp camp.

The Research Center by then had a darkroom to handle the extensive photographic records that Hugo Van Lawick had started for every chimp. It also had a botanical museum with all of Gombe's plant life named and explained, as well as a library in both Swahili and English, with books on animal behavior and Tanzanian history. The project had grown so large that Goodall, who was supervising all the scientific work, relinquished the nonscientific management to a pair of administrators, Emilie Bergman from Holland, and Etha Lohay, the first Tanzanian woman to go through national park ranger training.

In 1975 Gombe still lacked running water, electricity, and roads. And malaria continued to strike down many of the scientists who came to work there. Yet it seemed like Eden to many who reached the remote jungle camp, particularly the Stanford students. All of them had read Goodall's books. They knew by heart the names and temperaments of David Graybeard, Fifi, Flint, and Flo. Enthusiastically they accepted her routine, working a twelve-hour "nest to nest" cycle. They bathed in the cold waterfalls during the dry season and swam in the clean lake water during the rainy months. Rocks tumbled dangerously down the falls and carved out new streams in the winter.

The students moved beyond the camp area into distant parts of the park and modified the earlier picture of chimp life based largely on camp observations. They joined in keeping track of the different chimpanzees. First they learned to recognize each animal, and then they helped with the records—all kinds of records. At chimp camp they rigged up a pail attached to a long rope around a branch. When they wanted to weigh a chimp to chart his growth, they placed a banana in the pail. When the chimp climbed the rope to retrieve it, he was weighed on a scale hidden in the foliage.

They learned complicated scientific procedures at Cambridge and at Stanford that are very different from the way Goodall herself had worked in the early years of the project. The new methods called for the kind of technical precision that Louis Leakey had predicted would develop as primate ethology matured into a major science.

The new procedure meant days in the forest beginning at 5:00 A.M., when the alarm clock went off in the small huts near chimp camp. The students could still see the giant tropical moon through the two-inch wire mesh that was all that covered their windows as they got dressed in the dim light and donned their "Gombe shoes," special brown plastic sandals that they bought in Kigoma which are especially resistant to the damp. They made their way to the camp kitchen, breakfasted on coffee and bread, tossed together a couple of jelly sandwiches to take along for lunch, and hurried off to meet the Tanzanian guide who accompanied every student into the bush.

Each pair moved together, adhering strictly to the rules: they kept at least four and a half yards behind the chimps, never touched the animals, and always returned to the mess hall near the lake by 7:30 P.M. to be accounted for. Students never slept in the forest as Goodall had occasionally done. And they had plenty of company at night to mull over their adventures or share a bottle of local Kionyagi beer or Tanzanian gin.

Most of the students discovered currents within themselves that responded to the mysteries of the wilderness. Others became deeply concerned with the local villagers, who still arrived daily at the clinic—the same clinic Vanne Goodall had started in 1960. And everyone followed the events in the chimps' lives and contributed to keeping the daily record of observations that Goodall had maintained unbroken since 1963. She divided the observations into two categories: some observers watched whole groups of animals, noting many postures, gestures, or facial expressions as well as the phase of the sexual cycle of female chimps; others followed an individual animal, noting carefully where it went as it wandered through the reserve, what it ate, and whom it met.

Goodall had already described the general pattern of chimp behavior. Now she asked the students to collect information that might explain specific relationships between individual animals. She assigned all the students to special projects, such as observing the two brothers, Figan and Faben, who seemed especially close, or watching different pairs of mothers with their infants.

The students worked out an "ethogram" for each study, a list of behavior patterns that described the chimpanzee at each stage of its life. The ethogram was plotted onto a check sheet that each student brought along into the bush. Students also carried maps, so they could mark down exactly where the activities they described took place, and a tape recorder filled with silica gel, which prevented moisture from ruining it. Finally, each observer carried a stopwatch, the ethologist's indispensable tool.

Although each check sheet was different, they all had boxes for the students to tick off at special intervals. Some sheets called for thirty-second checks, some for intervals of five minutes. Most of the sheets called for a half hour's worth of observations, and a student might fill in several of those sheets during one day in the field.

But of course the check sheet could not account for everything that might happen. That was where the tape recorder came in. The observers described into it any impressions or curious events that did not fit in anywhere else. Back in camp, they would transcribe their taped observations onto note cards, which were triplicated and sent along to Stanford to undergo statistical analysis.

The detailed check sheets categorized thousands of hours of observation made by many different observers. Eventually, the observations fell into a pattern that was more precise and objective than any one person's narrative. Sometimes small details that different observers may have picked up fell into a pattern when so much data were seen together.

Collecting this kind of data demands patience. And the results are usually less startling than the observations Jane Goodall made when she first sighted the chimpanzees termiting, or hunting other animals, but they are very accurate and reliable. Occasionally something dramatic happened within a family that was exciting precisely because they now knew the history of that particular family. The implications of these revelations were and are just as important as the earlier discoveries in terms of what they reveal about chimpanzee behavior. Such a revelation occurred when Flo died.

· Goodall had first noticed Flo with her ragged ears and bulbous nose a decade earlier, and even then she had thought of her as old. Yet Flo had kept her dominant role in the community, even lording it over some of the male animals. During her later years she had traveled mostly with her youngest child, Flint, taking good care of him. She had also spent a lot of time with daughter Fifi and grandson Freud. Yet she still mixed with the larger community, where her sons Figan and Faben, who still came to her occasionally for comfort, had risen to dominance.

Then early in 1972, Flo stopped socializing outside the boundaries of her family. That summer proved especially dry at Gombe and the fruit trees did not produce their usual crop. Flo found less and less to eat. As her life ebbed, Flo grew so feeble that she could scarcely cover a hundred yards without having to lie down to rest. Years of chewing had so worn down her teeth that she could not eat bark, as many of the other hungry chimps were doing. And climbing the trees for green leaves was just too much for her. Finally, one day in August, Flo came to a small valley where she sank down to the ground, her head face down in a clear stream. With her at the time was eight-and-a-half-year-old Flint.

Flo might have survived longer in a lusher season. But she was old and her days numbered. The observers who had been watching this inevitable unwinding of her energies left the body where it had fallen in the stream for three days before they removed it. They spent the time, however, watching Flint.

Flint had shared his old mother's nest when she was dying. He had still been coming to her for grooming, or to beg a piece of food. Now, for the first day after her death, Flint hovered close to her body, only leaving it briefly to go to chimp camp nearby for a banana. During the day Flint approached the body gingerly, sniffed it, and once he even groomed the hair. That evening Flint climbed into an old nest that must have been one of the last ones they had shared.

On the third day of his orphanhood, Flint left Flo. He walked away from the stream, but kept looking back over his shoulder, even when she had long since passed from his sight. That night, for the first time since her death, Flint met his brother Figan, and nested close to him. But the next day he wandered off alone again. And for the next three days he returned to the stream where Flo's body had lain. Not until the seventh day of his vigil did Flint meet Fifi and Freud, with whom he spent the next three nights. But they wandered off, leaving him alone at the stream.

Gradually Flint's appetite failed and he began to shrink. As the observers watched, his once-bright eyes seemed to be sinking into his head. His movements became abrupt and nervous, then heavy and slow. He did not seem to have the will to build his own nest at night, but instead slept in old ones, probably those he had shared with his mother.

Flint remained where Flo had died, unable to find solace in either his sister or brothers. His condition deteriorated quickly and finally the human observers stepped in. At first they tried bringing him food, and they tried to help him emotionally by leading other chimpanzees, especially Fifi and Freud, to where he now lay unable to move. But he never responded. Twenty-two days after Flo's death, Flint sank into a coma. The observers injected him with a heart stimulant, but it was too late. At Flint's death, this small primate, whose whole life had been recorded onto data sheets that are now stored on three continents, lay beneath a man-made blanket, his hand in the hand of the man who had been his tracker. His autopsy did not reveal any serious organic problem. He had apparently died from grief.

In 1960, when Jane Goodall was getting established at Gombe, Dr. David Hamburg at Stanford University proposed the construction of an outdoor primate facility there where researchers would be able to perform controlled experiments with chimpanzees. The California facility opened in 1972 with a Gombe alumnus, Dr. Patrick McGinnis, as its coordinator.

Getting to Gombe, in Africa, the traveler passes through increasingly rugged primitive country. But to reach Stanford's Outdoor Primate Facility, one travels through the grounds of the Linear Accelerator, a physics' research installation two miles long, a curious contrast in the extremes of modern science. Signs warn of radioactivity, and all vehicles are checked as they enter and eventually approach high concrete walls, reminiscent of a medieval keep, but one from which grunts of chimpanzees challenge the accelerator's low hum.

Inside the observation center, on a sheltered deck, observers focus binoculars on the two large pie-shaped chimpanzee en-

Chimp: _____
Observer: _____
Day: _____ Month: _____ Year: _____
Time: _____ (Standard _____ Daylight _____)
Geographic locality: _____
Female chimp's bottom: M O ¼ ½ — 1 *
Time interval: _____

Temperature: _____
Barometric pressure: _____

cold ———— cool ———— mild ———— warm ———— hot
° (F. or C.)

Light level: _____
Precipitation: _____
Wind: _____
Wind direction: _____

dull ———— haze ———— cloudy-bright ———— bright
fog ———— drizzle ———— rain ———— snow
nil ———— light ———— mod. ———— strong
(blowing from…)

N
W E
S

Continuous watch for A. S. S. R.†							
Time	Beh. Code	Aux. Info.	Quad	Arm's Reach	?	Comments	Time
			N O				
01							01
02							02
03							03
04							04
05							05
06							06
07							07
08							08
09							09
10							10
--------							--------
60							60

Check sheet used at the Stanford Outdoor Primate Facility

Courtesy Patrick R. McGinnis

*The notation used for a female chimp in estrus: M (Maximal or rump in "flower"), O (Ovulation), followed by different times in the cycle.

†Behavior of the animal being studied is noted as A (Aggressive threat or attack), S (Sexual), S (Submissive), R (Reassurance).

closures, each encompassing an acre and a half of land. These are not Gombe chimps, although they were wild-born, and these animals do not live here as they would in the wild. But it is easier for observers here than in the forest, where the foliage often prevents sustained observations. These enclosures have no blind spots. The humans can observe the animals constantly, although the animals cannot see their observers. Inside their walls, the chimps have a place to play and things to do, but it is not a re-creation of the wild habitat. It does, however, offer the chimps enough space to act and react in a normal way.

The work at Stanford is tied in with the research at Gombe, but they use different methods. At Gombe the work is purely observational, but at Stanford the scientists can experiment. The conventional primate laboratory keeps primates in cages, some-what similar to keeping humans in solitary confinement. But years of association with the wild chimpanzees at Gombe had taught the California team how to simulate the natural habitat so that the chimps there have enough room for exercise and do not crowd each other.

The California team uses check sheets too, to monitor the behavior of their group of chimps. But they are especially interested in matching up the animals' behavior with their physio-logical responses. These chimps are trained to let a human take a small blood sample from their veins in exchange for food. The researchers can then scan the blood for hormonal changes, par-ticularly those changes which occur naturally in adolescence. Moreover, they also monitor the effects of injecting hormones into the chimps to see how it affects their behavior.

The scientists at Stanford come from various disciplines: psychiatry, ethology, biochemistry, and statistics. They believe that these studies will provide clues for research on human behavior. They are hopeful that this closest of our primate rela-tives may offer insights into our evolution, especially our under-standing of human behavioral biology.

Flint's decline followed a pattern identical to the way some people react to grief. Should this situation happen to a chimp at Stanford, they could monitor his hormones and find out how his blood changed chemically to make him lose his appetite and die. Flint's death is an important phenomenon.

But it is not the end of his story. With his absence, and Flo's, the balance of the whole Kikombe chimpanzee community changed. Figan and Faben remained dominant, but Fifi grew solitary. And poor Freud suffered particularly; after a lifetime of living in a large, friendly family, he was alone.

Goodall had watched other small chimps experience orphanhood, but the others had been much younger. Some had died, and others had adopted an older sister as a stepmother. Flint's death provokes many questions. Why did Flint, who was old enough to get along alone, succumb to grief? Did he suffer from too much mothering? Would be have survived had he found Fifi sooner, before he had sunk so far into the chasm of his misery? Knowing so much about Flint's history and the structure of his family, the researchers at Gombe were able to monitor the effect of these two deaths on the whole community. After fifteen years, all the data at Gombe had begun to pay off.

But today the darkroom is closed, the apparatus gone. The library books are in Dar es Salaam, eight hundred miles away. For the time being the Gombe Stream Research Center is closed, except for a few Tanzanian staff members who continue to make some observations under very limiting circumstances.

The staff had taken precautions against disease, inoculating newcomers against tropical ills. They had explained to everyone how to cope with surprise encounters with wild buffalo and snakes. But they could not have prepared for the events of May 19, 1975.

Late spring and the sun had already dried up the winter rains, leaving the forest fresh. Gombe was at that delicious balance in the tropical year when the remote lakeside is green and dry. The lake was placid after the winter storms. All was calm.

It was a Sunday evening, and the human population was asleep, except for the administrator, Emilie Bergman, who was up working late, her kerosene lamp burning in the window of her small hut on the slope. The first hint of trouble came at the beach where the Tanzanian staff lived. The boat that came out of the darkness surprised the park rangers when it spewed out a cargo of forty uniformed guerillas who carried machine guns, rifles, and pistols, and spoke French and Lingala, a dialect popular in Zaire, across the lake. The raiders roughed up the Africans, then demanded that they turn the white people over to them.

The Tanzanians refused and some of them risked their lives to sneak through the forest to warn as many people as possible of the danger. The commotion on the beach spread up the slope where other people were sleeping near chimp camp.

The raiders rushed onward to the light where Emilie Bergman was working. They ransacked her hut and grabbed her. Then they continued into another hut, where they surprised a young man. The sight of strangers speaking an unknown language startled him into shouts of "Help!" Two women students rushed in, only to fall along with him and Emilie Bergman into the hands of the guerillas, who bound them hand and foot and kidnapped them, taking along Gombe's only power boat as well. Those still at Gombe reported that the Research Center had been raided and that altogether three American students and a Dutch national had been kidnapped.

After a week, the soldiers rowed Barbara Smuts, one of the American women, the thirty-five miles back across Lake Tanganyika—a fifteen-hour trip—and deposited her on the lakeshore so that she could make her way into Kigoma. She brought with her the details of her capture and the demands of their captors. This ultimately led to difficult but successful negotiations. The other women were released first, and finally, at the end of August, the young man was freed too.

But the price was higher than any ransom. Gombe was exposed as too remote and too vulnerable to the tactics of this terrorist group. Goodall supervised the removal of all her data to the capital city of Dar es Salaam. Incomplete as it is, her work there and the work of her students has already revolutionized our view of both chimpanzee behavior and our perspective of ourselves.

At Gombe, meanwhile, ten Tanzanian trackers continue to

report on the activities of Fifi and Freud and the recent disappearance of Figan. Goodall visits the park from time to time, but always escorted now by a group of armed guards. She hopes that at least part of the research there will continue. If it cannot, she will continue to study animal behavior in other forest laboratories in Tanzania's national parks. As for the chimpanzees, they will continue living as they have always lived, unaware of how great their contribution has been to the science of primatology.

PART II

MOUNTAIN GORILLAS

Alan Root, National Geographic Society
Dian Fossey, amid the foliage at lower left, in the mountains of Rwanda, avoids staring at the gorilla that observes her.

4

Dian Fossey
in Rwanda

The wood fire burns all day and all night in the pit in front of
Dian Fossey's green-painted sheet-metal cabin. Moisture clings
to everything in this lush saddle area in the Virunga Mountains,
two hundred miles north of Lake Tanganyika and more than ten
thousand feet above the far-off sea. The fire dries her clothing,
heats her water, and helps ward off the pervasive chill. Rain falls
almost every day and thick mists swirl through the high valley,
obscuring nearby trees, the stream, and the other cabins. On
rare days when the sun breaks through, Dian Fossey steps out of
her cabin and is able to see the strangely flat cone of towering
Mount Visoke, bright against a deep blue sky. On these days the
Karisoke Research Center is one of the most beautiful places on
earth.

Fossey is close to six feet tall, a handsome woman with a
high forehead and open face. She wears her thick black hair in
a braid over her shoulder. At dusk, her dog, Cindy, at her feet,
typing in the orange glow of a kerosene lamp, she seems at
peace. She keeps her own counsel and is happiest alone with
Cindy, her two tamed ravens, and a pet Sykes' monkey. She spent
her first two years in these mountains just that way, apparently
immune to the woes of solitude. Those who have worked with
her since then marvel at her inner strength and determination,
look on her in awe, and always remark upon her wry sense of
humor.

In 1975 her two-room cabin was one of a half dozen green huts that blend into the alpine landscape. They shelter a pair of African trackers, her African camp staff, and science students and specialists from the United States and England, who work with her from time to time. The Gorilla Project is a decade old now, and though this is not her first camp, Fossey has been in Rwanda the greatest part of the time. But Camp Visoke is no Gombe. It has not grown so large and probably never will see more than a handful of scientists at one time.

The eight Virunga volcanoes that crown the equator in East Africa—spanning the boundaries of Rwanda, Zaire, and Uganda —are forbidding. Here legend speaks of the Great Spirit Gonga who, in fierce struggles with the other spirits, spits out lava and fire in his fury. The battle goes on. As recently as 1958, fresh lava erupted from the base of nearby Mount Nyamuragira, adding new scars to the older, overgrown pits that mar the unsettled mountain crust.

The scientists who work in this damp chill are subdued. They spend long hours quietly observing the giant apes, tirelessly analyzing the data they collect. Fossey directs the camp, shunning publicity for herself, yet at the same time hoping to broadcast to the world the desperate plight of the mountain gorilla. She sets the mood here, as somber as the slow-moving black giants she watches.

The mountain gorillas are new to man. Our Western zoos are full of the captive lowland species, *Gorilla gorilla gorilla,* from Gabon and the Cameroons. They too are endangered, but they are not losing ground as rapidly as the mountain dwellers, *Gorilla gorilla beringei*. The mountain gorillas are slightly smaller than the lowland species, have longer hair and a longer palate, and they do not share their forest with chimpanzees as the other gorillas do. They have adapted to a different habitat, and per- haps have evolved a different way of behaving.

Whatever this behavior, it was almost completely mysterious until 1959 when an American ethologist, George B. Schaller, spent a year wandering among the volcanoes in what was then

Albert National Park, a tract forty-eight miles long that had been declared a gorilla sanctuary in 1933. Schaller began his brief study at just about the same time Jane Goodall was setting up camp in Gombe.

In the months he spent there, Schaller traveled without a gun, heedless of the tales still highly popular that Du Chaillu had spread a century earlier. Schaller returned from his wanderings in good health, and reported the discovery of a highly social and very gentle animal.

Far away from the Congo, in Louisville, Kentucky, Dian Fossey, who was head of the occupational therapy unit at a hospital for crippled children, read his account. Fossey had felt an extraordinary sympathy for animals all her life, and admits that even as a child she felt more at home with animals than with people. She is particularly attracted to what she feels is the freedom wild animals enjoy.

Fossey rode show horses during her college days in California, where she spent several years studying veterinary medicine before she switched to physiotherapy. And it was Kentucky's famous horses, as much as the hospital job, that brought her to Louisville. But when she read Schaller's description of gorillas, she decided that she had already spent too much time waiting. She had always wanted to visit Africa to see the animals totally free, and realizing that "procrastination is the root of never doing," she borrowed enough money to spend two months on safari in the fall of 1963.

Part of her African adventure took her to the Virunga volcanoes, where she was lucky enough to meet the English photographer Alan Root and his wife, who were studying and photographing gorillas there. The Roots showed her how to watch the great apes, and in return she entertained them at an improvised tea, fourteen thousand feet above sea level. She set a table of logs between huge volcanic boulders that she cushioned in yards of soft moss, then decorated with garlands of wild orchids and violets.

She loved the country as much as she loved the animal life, and she intended to return. She continued north to Olduvai, where

Louis Leakey was working at his dig. Shy then, or perhaps intimidated by the great man when she met him for the first time, she did not even mention her interest in the wild gorilla.

On her return to Louisville, she poured out the drama of her safari in the Sunday supplement of the *Courier-Journal*. She described the sheer terror she had felt when she first heard the gorilla's air-rending shriek. She also described its footprint, which swallowed up her own foot in its size 9½ boot. But she went on to discuss the plight of this rare giant, and begged that it be saved.

When Leakey next found himself in the United States, he headed for Kentucky to find the woman who had written so passionately about the greatest of all the apes. At the hospital he put it to her bluntly. He asked Dian Fossey to attempt a long-term study of gorillas in much the same way Jane Goodall was successfully studying chimpanzees.

Leakey had already sent two young women to try the task, but neither had been able to track the animals. One of them had been vanquished by the unhealthy climate, and both had been frustrated by their fleeting glimpses of gorillas that never lasted long enough to record. After a year, all that either of them had to report were collections of day-old nests and piles of food and dung, so they had given up. Leakey believed that now he had found in thirty-five-year-old Dian Fossey a potential scientist tough enough for the job.

Fossey responded to Leakey's challenge immediately. She quit her job and set out for California, where her family lived, to say good-bye. But scientific research costs a lot of money, and Fossey could not leave for Africa as soon as she had hoped. While Leakey plied his usual sources for funds, Fossey waited impatiently, but used the time to confer with the experts at Stanford's Primate Facility. At Leakey's suggestion, she also took the opportunity to get rid of her appendix. It would be a messy kind of emergency up in the mountains, he explained.

After what seemed an eternity but was in fact only three months, she left for Gombe to visit Jane Goodall and to see how the research was set up there. She arrived in Zaire at Christmastime 1966. Fossey headed for the same national park where Schaller had worked; where Carl Akeley (who had convinced the Belgians to set aside the park in 1921) lies buried. But seven years had brought change to what had been, in Schaller's day, the Belgian Congo. Three new nations now governed the Virunga volcanoes, and relations among them were unstable. In fact, the borders between Zaire and Uganda were sealed.

The mountain gorillas, of course, did not respect these borders. Fossey also tried to ignore politics as she began to roam the meadows and wooded slopes around Kabara, seeking the gorillas she had read so much about. The national park had been well run, and the gorillas who lived there at first ran and screamed when they spotted her, but soon they let her observe them from a short distance without fleeing. At the end of six months she felt that she had made a good start and was well on her way to winning the trust of these wild animals, a true habituation of them to a human being. She knew that Jane Goodall had spent as much time habituating the more outgoing chimpanzees, so she was pleased to have made so much more progress than the earlier researchers.

But just at this point, political turmoil swept the lowlands of Zaire. The director of the park felt he could not ensure her safety, and he ordered her down from the mountainside. She was placed under house arrest for two weeks, during which time she lived in fear both for her life and for the future of her work.

Unable to remain helpless before the unknown any longer, Fossey took her own action. She explained to the six Congolese soldiers stationed at her house that in order to obey their law, she had to register her car. And for that she needed cash, so she asked them to escort her to the border town of Kisoro, where she could cash a check. Leaving her supplies in Zaire, she tucked her data, some personal belongings, and a flock of chickens into the Land Rover. She also piled in her six guards, who seemed to accept the company of chickens as just more proof that this gorilla-watching American was crazy.

Once inside her car, she sped across the border into Uganda. There she gained refuge at the Travellers Rest Hotel, a beautiful lodge at the foot of the Virunga volcanoes, whose German-born proprietor, Walter Baumgartel, was another defender of the endangered wild gorilla. The guards were escorted back to Zaire, and Fossey was officially labeled *persona non grata* and warned that should she so much as step over the border again, she'd be shot.

Equipment gone; six months' hard work habituating the gorillas gone; yet the setback only spurred her on. By fall she had set up her present camp above beautiful Lake Kivu, near the town of Gisenyi, on the slopes of Mount Visoke in the more friendly political climate of Rwanda.

Its national park, the Parc des Volcans, had been more casually run than the park land to the north. No hut awaited her when she climbed to ten thousand feet above sea level, and her Land Rover could only follow a rough road to the eight-thousand-foot mark. There she still has to leave it. At this height, with the air thin and breathing difficult, she climbs on foot, winding around and around a three-mile trail to reach the saddle area where she has her camp, only five miles from her original campsite in Zaire.

The park was poorly controlled. Poachers and herdsmen ignored the law and trespassed nonchalantly to seek grazing for their cows and to hunt wild red duikers (miniature antelopes) for their dinners. Some even hunted gorillas, remembering their ancient rites that called for gorilla testicles, ear lobes, tongues, and digits to complete magical potions.

Appalled at the wanton murder of the gorillas, as well as the destruction of the ground cover upon which not only the gorilla but the wild elephants and buffalo also depended, Fossey began to wage her private war against the human predators. She has succeeded, and there is more discipline in the park now. She still makes random patrols, and when she sees traps, she destroys them. She has also pulled down scores of poachers' huts and has not hesitated to shoot trespassing cows which were devouring the precious ground cover.

Fossey had no good companion like Vanne Goodall to set up a clinic and establish contact with the villagers for her. Instead, she has had to manage by herself, facing the complex difficulties of coping with people who speak a patchwork of languages. She is at home in English, and has mastered everyday Swahili, the unofficial language of many Africans. But it is no one's first language, and she does not speak the local Kinyarwanda, nor is she comfortable in French, the official language of the country, left over from Belgian colonial rule.

Language and cultural barriers still confront her. She finds herself engaged in a battle of priorities in which twentieth-century science and conservation values confront both ancient tribal lore and the timeless economics of poverty.

Rwanda is one of the most densely populated countries in Africa. Its hungry people keep cultivating land, pushing the wildlife farther up the mountainsides. The people want fields to grow their maize and potatoes. They do not understand why the rich volcanic soil within the park should be left untilled. The hungry are not interested in conservation, and they find it hard to sympathize with the fate of the animals they have feared and hunted for generations.

Yet the farmers are only part of the threat. Tall Tutsi herdsmen in their long white caftans carrying seven-foot staffs still shepherd their cows inside the park and let them forage the precious ground cover. The Tutsi do not eat these cows or milk them. Instead they covet their elegant long horns, a sign of wealth, and allow these hungry status symbols to destroy the gorillas' vegetation and upset the ecological balance in the park.

There are also the Bahutu, who do not hunt gorillas, but who cut down the precious slow-growing trees in search of beehives. And finally, the Batwa pygmies, who set vicious rope snares to catch the duiker. The snares just as easily trap a gorilla, which may hang, suffering, for days before it dies or is set free. With her *panga,* a broad-bladed knife, in hand, Fossey sweeps away the illegal traps and on at least one occasion she put on a Halloween mask and frightened the superstitious hunters right out of the park.

She is a hero to conservationists, the awe of Rwandese officialdom, and a respected enemy of the poachers she is fighting. Those who know her admire her, some more than others. One of her African employees at Camp Karisoke sent a lock of her hair to a witch doctor across the border in Zaire, which came back in a love potion. He hoped that magic would help him win this awesome woman, or at least understand her.

The Rwandese may not all share Fossey's passionate interest in gorillas. But they admire her hard-nosed enforcement of the law, perhaps because they sense that her dedication to gorillas goes beyond the law.

Her Rwandese staff spread the news that she had habituated eight different gorilla groups, which she numbered One through Eight for identification. Within these groups, each of which contains between two and sixteen different animals, she became familiar with many individuals and gave them names. Some she called in Swahili, like Rafiki, which means friend. Others she called by English nicknames, like the large male, Peanuts, the gentle giant who had been the first to reach out and touch her hand.

The Rwandese knew that Fossey tried to contact the gorillas every day for fear that any interruption might impede the slow task of habituating them. Yet they risked asking her to help them save an infant gorilla that had been illegally trapped and sold to a West German zoo because they understood her compassion for these animals. The baby animal was dying, and so Fossey agreed to interrupt her observations to try to save its life, understanding all along that it would still eventually have to make the trip to Germany.

On a cold, misty spring morning, with the frost still brittle on the ground, Dian Fossey pushed through the curtains of fog to lead a single file of bearers up the slippery mountain trail. Her face was red with exertion from the four-hour hike, but her eyes sparkled with excitement. Behind her a party of Africans carried a small child's playpen with the top boarded over. In front of her the African staff waited expectantly at the cabin door.

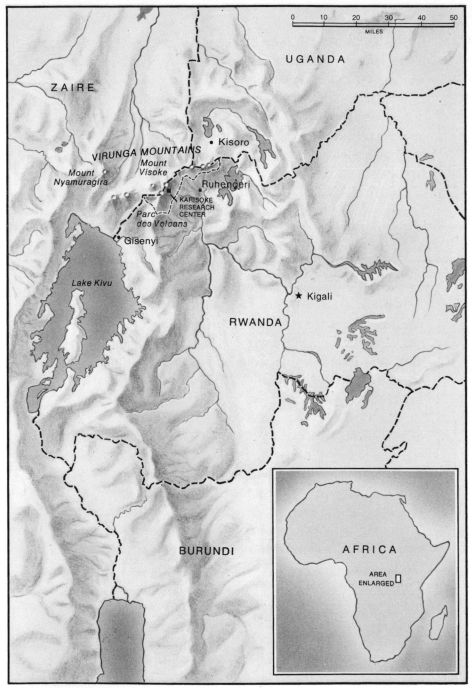

Karisoke Research Center in Rwanda

George Buctel

She had instructed them to carry out some rather odd orders: to transform the second room in her cabin from a place of books and curios into a forest sanctuary. A huge piece of a tree stood against one wall, and vines and leaves covered the floor.

She watched the playpen for a moment as the bearers set it down gently in the room. Then she closed the door and pried off the boards from the top. Two shiny black eyes peered up at her, and then the small sixteen-month-old male, whom she instantly named Coco, escaped from his prison and scurried to the top of the "tree," meeting the unexpected phenomenon of a ceiling. Later, she recalled, he climbed down and sat on the floor, staring out through the large glass window toward the mountaintop. Looking at what had been so recently his home, he sobbed piteously, eventually crying himself to sleep.

Just one week after that the nursery doubled. Two-year-old Pucker Puss, a female, arrived to join Coco, who by this time had lapsed into a high fever, precariously teetering on the verge of death. Twenty-six days stuffed inside a wire cage where he could neither sit nor stand seemed to have broken his spirit. Pucker Puss was also in bad shape. The forest nursery became an infirmary as Fossey put to use her earlier veterinary training as well as her years at the children's hospital, mixing formulas and medicating the baby animals around the clock. Slowly the small gorillas grew to trust her and began to improve. After sixty-nine days in her care, they were well enough to travel; reluctantly she let them be carried off to their European zoo.

Rearing the young gorillas even for just a few months was a special treat. Like all small animals, they were engaging and loving. Perhaps small apes are even more enchanting because they look and act so much like human babies. With these sick charges, Fossey could temporarily break one of the iron rules of scientific research. She could stroke and even fondle these wild animals because there was no danger that they would mature and turn their affection into death hugs, or at the least become so tamed that they would no longer be "wild" and therefore worthless as a source of study.

The two infants which had been thrust upon her had no future in the mountains, so the rules no longer held. But they offered her an unexpected dividend. From them she discovered how infant apes learn to eat, and she also began to grasp the meanings of the different sounds they made. She had gained an important skill. Afterward she could actually "communicate" with the wild gorillas in their own "language."

By this time she had been in the Virunga Mountains for several years, and Louis Leakey urged her to go to study in Cambridge, England, as he had urged Jane Goodall earlier. Leakey himself had had to fight the scientific establishment and he knew the value of the right credentials. With a doctorate in her hand, Fossey might be called a maverick or an eccentric, but she could never be called an amateur.

She went to England and found the ancient university town of Cambridge as wet and cold as her beloved mountains, but otherwise it was too remote from what she now considered home. She missed her work and worried about what the farmers and poachers might be doing while she was away. Less anxious for a degree than Leakey had been for her, Fossey left Cambridge before she received her Ph.D. But she is still working toward it and is in close touch with her colleagues there from her mountain camp.

Going back seemed to take longer than arriving the first time. Once home, she tried to re-establish her ties at once. She spent six long days searching the almost perpendicular mountain slopes, climbing high into the alpine forests and crossing valleys thick with nettles and wild bamboo before she found the gorilla groups she had habituated. She especially looked for the young male blackback, Peanuts, and the old male, Rafiki, whose back hairs had turned white with maturity, earning him the title of silverback. When they met again, they accepted her, and she knew she could continue where she had left off. With renewed zeal she made her way through the swirling mists to join the wild gorillas who still remembered her. Occasionally she leaves Africa on visits, but these mountains have become her home.

Her working day is still very much as it was in 1967. Up before dawn in the small cabin, she cooks her breakfast and puts on thermal underwear, flannel shirt, jeans, and an army surplus jacket. In a haversack she packs her writing material, gloves, and a nylon raincoat in case the drizzle should become a downpour.

Her African trackers take turns noting the whereabouts of the groups she is watching. They mark the sleeping sites of the different groups on a map so that she does not have to waste time searching for them. Cindy accompanies her until she finds the gorillas. Then, on a leash, the trackers take the dog back to camp, leaving Fossey alone with the apes.

She is always careful to approach the gorillas softly, crawling or crouching. She has learned that wild gorillas find any creature taller than themselves disturbing. She makes her presence known to them and then sits down a few feet away, watching. She remains silent, for she knows that her voice may startle them. And she hardly ever carries binoculars or a camera anymore, for the shiny glass upsets some of them. Above all else, she wants the gorillas to remain as they were and accept her as just another forest creature so that she can uncover the secrets of their lives.

When they groom themselves, she raises her hand to scratch her own head noisily, showing that she too enjoys a good scratch. Should they look warily at her, she may fold her arms across her chest, a sign that indicates she is submissive and no threat to the four-hundred-pound males, and not asking for trouble.

She moves with them through the grass, six feet high and thick as a cornfield with tiny colored flowers, clusters of white and yellow members of the daisy family. When the gorillas stop to munch on wild celery stalks, she grabs a juicy clump and pretends to chew it, making loud noises to show that she finds it as delicious as they do. When they echo a resounding belch that signals that the food is good, and there is plenty of it, she answers in a belly belch herself. The animals accept her presence among them and let her continue moving with them through the day.

The gorillas eat in the morning, then travel a while. They take a nap at noon, if there is sun, in a warm glade. While the gorillas doze, Fossey takes notes and records everything she has witnessed in a peculiar shorthand she has evolved. Playtime follows the siesta, and now the infant gorillas sometimes approach this strange primate—explore her haversack, her gloves, her thermos and notebook, pull at her shoelaces, and maybe even groom the burrs from her white socks. The infants race up and down the tall tree trunks that their parents now disdain. They gambol with each other in the high grass and test the patience of the adult members of the group.

Fossey stays with the gorillas until they've nested down on the ground or in low tree branches. Then she returns to her camp cabin, a cosy room filled with bright red pillows, shelves of African art objects, and gorilla lore. She sups quietly and may take out her typewriter and translate the notes she has jotted down during the day. Sometimes she studies her information or adds to the photographic file—a portrait gallery of ninety gorillas she has known over the years.

From these pictures Fossey has made noseprints of each animal. Sometimes she uses a telephoto lens to get close-ups of their faces. The gorilla's flat, broad nose is marked by sworls between the nostrils and the upper lip. Noseprints are as distinctive to gorillas as earprints are to elephants, and fingerprints to humans. Fossey and her trackers use them to identify the individual apes they encounter in their daily trips into the forest. Other evenings Fossey may puzzle over the gorilla fossils she has been collecting since she arrived in the mountains, for she is as interested in gorilla evolution and gorilla history as she is in the ape's present adaptation to its environment.

Other scientists have joined her in the last few years, some for a few months, some for a year or two. The presence of more people has obliged her to vary her routine. As administrator, she has to take time off to direct their work, if they are students, and to work with them if they are specialists like the botanist from Missouri who spent three months at Karisoke in the spring of 1975.

She has not tamed the gorillas, nor does she want to. She

has not tamed the volcanic mountains either. Life there still holds dangers to which she is constantly alert. Cape buffalo herds move through the trees and one gored a student. Fossey saved the student's life using her medical ingenuity. Another unfortunate visitor was trampled to death while trying to photograph one of the elephants that move silently and treacherously in the forest. Fossey broke a leg on the mountain slopes in 1974 and treated herself until she felt strong enough to risk the trip down to the hospital in Ruhengeri. Occasionally a student gets lost at night in the forest. Then she sends for Rwandese villagers to help scan the territory. Any accident or illness is doubly dangerous because help is so far away.

Yet these dangers were there when Fossey arrived, and they are familiar now, and so less fearful to her. She has learned to ward off poachers, to work with the local government, and to respond in medical emergencies. Above all, she is at home with these free-roaming animals. Her research is beginning to bear fruit as her mastery of new methods of collecting data enables her to slowly unveil the texture of gorilla life.

5

Scientist at Work

Several years passed after Fossey established camp in Rwanda before she hiked back the five miles through wet undergrowth across the border into Zaire. She wanted to visit her old field camp in the Kabara Meadow to see what had become of those first gorillas she had begun to habituate. Hidden in the thick mists, she could find only half of the animals she remembered. She returned to the Karisoke Center more determined than ever to save the surviving mountain gorilla from extinction.

What scientists find is usually what they are looking for, and they choose their tools to suit their goals. Fossey has been looking for ways to preserve the free-ranging gorillas. In order to do that she had to take a census, find out how they lived in harmony with their environment, and how often the females gave birth. After she crossed the first hurdle—habituating the gorillas —she went to study ethology at Cambridge. There she learned to supplement her intuition with scientific procedures. Now she works meticulously with a small, well-chosen staff. Measuring everything that can possibly affect the gorillas' lives, she submits their patiently accumulated data to statistical analysis, just as Goodall's chimp team had at Gombe.

It takes only a week or two in the mountains with Fossey to be able to recognize each gorilla individually. She and her staff know the permanent residents by name, and when a newcomer appears, they spot it right away and add it to the census. So far she has counted fewer than ninety animals in the immediate area around her camp. Others estimate that there cannot be more than a thousand mountain gorillas in the entire range. She has used the maps made by her trackers to plot the territory each group moves within to estimate the total gorilla population.

She sits in her small cabin examining a map. She had it made from a 1958 aerial photograph of the Virunga volcanoes, and she has superimposed a grid over it. When she holds the map up, it is like looking through a screened window onto the distant peaks. Using many copies of enlarged sections of the gridded map, she and her staff have plotted the travels of known gorilla groups. Overlaying flat squares onto an aerial photograph of mountains is, of course, slightly inaccurate. But the mountains are so incredibly thick with vegetation that pacing them in the traditional way would have been impossible. By marking down where the gorillas stop to eat, Fossey has been able to discover which foods they depend on, and she passes this information on to the park authorities, who are ultimately responsible for the animals' survival.

She spends her days hip deep in dripping vines and leaves, often in pouring rain, marking down where the gorillas are and what they are doing. In contrast, she spends her evenings in the orange glow of a kerosene lamp, transferring these movements onto a graph. Slowly, as the days blend into weeks, the ruled lines begin to show an amoebic shape. The close contact with the rich smell of damp, decaying leaves, and the overpowering pungent odor of the gorillas is transformed into cold mathematical evidence.

Fossey has broken down this area of the mountains into six vegetation zones, through which the gorilla groups journey. The zones vary according to both the altitude and the herbs and trees that grow within them. Happily, more than half the park is made up of rolling alpine meadow, the saddle area between three fourteen-thousand-foot-high mountains. Here grow the two trees that the gorillas depend on most, the hypericum, which looks something like an American oak tree and produces a small almond-sized fruit, and the hagenia, a tree unique to Central Africa. The hagenia has an especially thick trunk and its heavy boughs branch out very low and grow horizontal to the ground. Giant ferns and vines encircle the hagenia, and soft liverwort moss wraps itself around the boughs. From higher branches, old-man's-beard, a hanging lichen, decorates the trees like bridal veils. The gorillas play in the hagenia branches and eat the vines and moss.

Slightly higher up the slopes is a flattish terrain elephant high in stinging nettles. They choke off all the undergrowth and make the land almost impenetrable to humans. The gorillas love the nettles and eat them whole, their mouths and fingers so tough that they do not seem to feel the needle-like spines.

Fossey has mapped the nettle patches and the frequent sharp ridges that break off abruptly into deep ravines. On the ridges the gorillas enjoy sweet blackberries; they love to loll in the sun like ancient Romans, eating lazily. They stretch out a hand to grab some berries and dangle them greedily into their open mouths. They pluck these fruits almost daintily, rather than stuff them into their mouths, as they do with leaves and stems. Fossey has singled out the slopes that support the vernonia trees, although they make up less than 4 percent of the gorillas' range. The vernonia's wide branches provide a haven for gorillas. It is here they build their nests and here the infants play. The vernonia is a favorite gorilla food, all of it. The apes reach up and eat the flowers, the leaves, and then break away the rotting bark and suck the juicy pith at the tree's core. Peeling and sucking, the gorillas are destroying these generous trees which, unlike most of the others, are very slow to grow again.

Fossey has also tracked gorillas into the highest alpine regions where the ground cover is thin and many saplings grow. Herds of elephant and buffalo also forage here. But gorillas hate to share their food, even with other gorillas, and they avoid using grazed-over areas like these, opting for untouched patches of wild celery, galium vines, and ground herbs.

From the group to the individual, Fossey's work is a seesaw movement. She needs to know the habits of the group, but she also seeks to understand why lone silverbacks carve out their own ranges. To satisfy both aims, she had narrowed her focus to a typical group, which she has studied intensely for almost seven years.

Group Four has grown and shrunk since she first met its members. Some animals have died, some wandered off, and new infants have been born to swell the ranks. Yet Group Four is fairly stable, like most gorilla groups. Gorillas, unlike chimpanzees, travel together in small clusters. They do not seek to mingle in a larger community, but keep to a small, well-structured social unit that is peculiar to gorillas. It is not a family, although it does contain mothers with their babies, but something other than blood ties holds the animals together.

It is probably the charismatic personality of the leader. Each gorilla group is led by a great silverbacked male, a full-grown animal that is almost six feet tall when he stands erect. The back of his body is covered with a saddle of white hair that contrasts sharply with the black hair covering the rest of him. With his outstretched arms, he can span eight feet, but despite his great size, he is usually a gentle, benevolent despot. Absolute, he commands his lieutenants, perhaps smaller silverbacked males, but more often younger blackbacked males who are full grown but not as old as the leader.

The rest of Group Four is made up of juveniles, smaller gorillas who are newly independent of their mothers but not full grown, and the females with their small, dependent infants.

Fossey has patiently tracked the ten to seventeen members of Group Four and mapped their movements. She has discovered that they do have a very precise home range, about seven square miles. She has watched the home range vary, gradually, as the leader explores new territory on its borders. She has also discovered that the home ranges of other gorilla groups overlap Group Four's, causing intermittent clashes between them.

Group Four does not like intruders. But instead of actually

driving others out, they discourage them from entering in the first place. One of their ploys is to deliberately overgraze the border area to make it seem as if all the food is gone. Another tack is to build their nests very close together, giving the impression of vast numbers and a united front.

But there is plenty of food around in this cool, humid mountain forest, and all the gorillas seem to know it. Farther down, where agriculture has replaced forest, the gorillas have been killed off by hunters, or have moved higher up. Where females have been killed, the gorillas do not get a chance to reproduce and so their numbers have dwindled even more. Because there is no food shortage, the gorillas do not have to travel as much as they actually do each day to find food. As Fossey plotted their travels, she wondered why they move about so much. Is the traveling an end in itself? Is it a pleasure for them, or a form of exercise? Why does Group Four zigzag, skipping one succulent hagenia tree for its twin eight hundred yards farther up the slope? She has puzzled over this and offers some explanations.

Mountain gorillas are intelligent animals who are especially well adapted to their forest. Although they do not use tools to get any of their food, as some chimpanzee cousins do, it is probably because the food they like is abundant without their having to make any effort. Moving, however, affords them protection from human hunters, who have been their most constant enemy. Keeping on the move also enables them to look out for other possible dangers—the arrival of migrant gorillas, or a hungry leopard, as well as man.

Their wanderings may also be one of the ways in which they help sustain the plant life that they need to survive. They never overgraze an area. The one tree they are destroying, the vernonia, is unusual in its very slow regeneration. The gorillas need vast amounts of vegetation to fill their great hanging stomachs, but just any food won't do. They choose quite carefully what they eat, and the order in which they eat it, as though they know what will help them digest it all properly.

Fossey has become expert at observing, recording, and interpreting gorilla behavior. But she is now concerned with why gorillas eat the way they do and, aware of her own scientific limitations, she has invited specialists, particularly botanists and experts in parasitology, to come to the Karisoke Center and use their specialized knowledge to study the relationship between gorillas and their environment.

The first to arrive, in the spring of 1975, was Dr. William D'Arcy, a botanist from the Missouri Botanical Gardens. D'Arcy surveyed the plant life of the Virunga volcanoes and collected specimens, some four thousand of them, which he eventually sent back to St. Louis for further study. At the same time he focused on the particular vegetation popular with the apes. He distilled more than twenty of their favorite foods to discover how much water they contain, as well as the nutritional content. Because gorillas in the wild almost never drink, it is especially important to find their source of water. He also observed the gorillas as they ate, overcoming an initial apprehension when he first met the enormous animals. He tried to figure out why they were eating what they ate, and when they ate it.

D'Arcy's tools included a very delicate Beecker balance scale, borrowed from a defunct gold mine that had once used it to measure gold dust, and a plant drier he rigged up himself to reduce his plant specimens in order to mount them on a page. The scale was simple enough to operate. The plant drier, however, proved an unexpected hazard.

His first effort to construct the drier inside the small cabin that Fossey offered him as living-office space ended when he set the drier atop the ubiquitous kerosene stove. The drier got too hot, the stove caught fire, and the whole cabin was in flames before they had time to remove anything from it. Fossey and D'Arcy managed to escape. But remote on the high slope, all they could do then was watch helplessly alongside the African staff as fire consumed the entire cabin, along with D'Arcy's research and his belongings.

That was the first try. While Fossey set to work immediately directing and helping rebuild the cabin, D'Arcy set up another plant drier on top of the outdoor pit fire. He was especially interested in discovering the source of certain nutrients in the gorillas' diet. Eventually he found a small gray snail beneath the nettle's leaves, which he thinks provides a needed element in their diet. He also noted that gorillas seem to have a penchant, perhaps a need, for sweets.

When the blackberries are ripe, the gorillas seem to know in advance and make their way to the ridges where they grow. Fossey wondered if they signaled to each other the news of such events. This led her to study another aspect of gorilla behavior, vocalizations.

Ever since she had cared for the small orphans Coco and Pucker Puss, Fossey had been interested in the complex vocalizations gorillas make. She noticed when she first arrived in Rwanda that the gorillas there seemed louder than those she had left behind in Zaire. She deduced that these gorillas still lived in terror of hunters and poachers in what was then poorly policed park land. They were screeching in alarm. She knew that George Schaller had been able to distinguish nine separate gorilla sounds. Going on from there, with more complex equipment, Fossey has distinguished another seven.

Using Group Four again as her study unit, Fossey spent forty months at it, a total of 2,255 hours (all field work, as a rule, is measured in "contact hours"). Arising at dawn, she found the gorilla group. Using a battery-operated tape recorder, she identified different kinds of sounds, and the different animals who made them. Then, with a Kaye-Sonogram machine, she later made "spectrograms" from the tapes. These are picture images of sound. They look very much like the up-and-down lines printed on an electrocardiogram. The sounds appear as patterns, each pattern representing a different call. Indeed, it is theoretically possible to use these tapes to make voiceprints of the individual animals as unique, probably, as the noseprints she has collected.

The sounds reveal a great deal about gorilla social life. Fossey recorded the call of infant gorillas to their mothers, a sound heard often from infants, but never heard again after the age of three. She transferred all the data from her tapes onto a chart and produced a picture of a primate society of outspoken males which vocalize in proportion to their place in the hierarchy, a social structure something like that of the chimps. The Alpha silverback male is the noisiest, the young blackbacks much quieter, and the quietest of all are the females. Fossey also discovered that a lot of this vocalizing is two-way communication. A gorilla's grunt demands, and receives, a response. The spectrograms prove the complexity of the ape's social system.

As the sonogram identifies the gorilla's cries of pleasure and distress, so does the Beecker scale sort out the nutrients in their foods, and the gridded map trace their wanderings. But just as the amoeba-like pattern on the map cannot reflect the damp smell of humus in the underbrush, and the scale cannot show the taste of wild berries, the sonogram does not reflect the sound of quiet. Alone with the gorillas beneath the hagenia trees, Fossey has felt their terror at the approach of poachers. She has read the penetrating sign they give of utter silence, followed by flight, and the dispersal of the entire gorilla group.

6

A Sunny Day

Morning

As the early sun's warm rays dissolve the thin haze on the ground beneath the hagenia tree, it looks as if this will be one of those glorious days in the mountains. The human observers crawling through the deep meadow grass are optimistic, their raincoats out of sight in their haversacks. One of them is new to Camp Visoke, so when they reach the slope where Group Four bedded down twelve hours earlier, they crouch low, out of sight behind a tree.

They watch silently as, one after another, the animals stretch in their nests, greeting the dawn. A small bird that looks like a North American sparrow watches with them for a while, then seems to forget the apes as it picks its breakfast with a pink beak. Except for the infants with their mothers, the thirteen gorillas sleep alone, scattered about in the thick ground cover or in the low branches of the hagenia tree.

Flossie, an adult female whom Dian Fossey has known for several years, is resting close to where the humans hide. With her is Titus, who was born last year, white-skinned and naked before his skin darkened and the black hair grew in thick. Today he is a miniature of his elders, save for the small fluff of white fur at his rump. Nearby, Flossie's older daughter, three-year-old Cleo, is moving in her own nest.

Infants like Titus depend on their mothers for food, and will nurse until they are almost two. He also needs her for transportation. He clung to her stomach when he was very small, and later on he learned to ride jockey-style like a young chimpanzee. When they reach three, young gorillas fall into another category. As juveniles, like Cleo, between the ages of three and five, they move about independent of their mothers for long stretches at a time. Yet they still return to her once in a while and try to sleep near her at night.

By the time a gorilla reaches the age of six, it is a young adult. Gorillas are sexually dimorphic, which means that the males grow to be much larger than the females, and have a different behavior pattern. At six, some males already weigh well over a hundred and fifty pounds, although they are still not finished growing. They are like adolescents in human society.

The female gorilla, like the female chimp, arrives at social maturity abruptly, usually when she is seven and gives birth to her first infant. She behaves like a juvenile until her infant is born. Then she suddenly becomes a solicitous mother and is accepted as an adult within the group.

The male gorilla goes through an adolescence much more distinctive than the male chimpanzee's. As blackbacks, between the ages of six and nine, young gorillas serve as guards and sentries for the silverback. They will not be mature until they develop their own white hair along the saddle of their heavily muscled backs, and the great sagittal crest becomes prominent on their heads, giving them the helmeted look of ancient Greek warriors. As silverbacks, they can rise to become the Alpha male of their group, remain content as seconds in command, or wander off as loners and eventually entice some females from an established group in order to form their own.

Females have their own hierarchy and argue noisily among themselves when they assert rank. Flossie starts barking hoarsely at a younger, childless female who is approaching her nest, and sends the smaller ape scurrying. Females often quarrel among themselves, screeching and barking over what they are eating, or reacting to how their offspring play together, but they never really fight.

At the moment, Flossie seems to be at the top of the female hierarchy because of Titus. When Fossey first observed her, Flossie was a lowly juvenile like the young female she just chased off. At that time the other females used her as an "aunt," or baby sitter, letting Flossie care for their young while they groomed themselves or ate. But the arrival of Cleo changed all that and shifted Flossie right to head status. Gradually, as Cleo grew, Flossie lost her position. But the arrival of Titus brought her back to the top again. All the gorillas, male and female, like babies. The newest member of the group is always the object of deep curiosity and consideration. The mothers take advantage of their new importance by demanding a better place to sit, nudging a lower gorilla to move over, and making a childless female baby-sit for her.

A nose-to-nose encounter with a 400-pound gorilla in the wild becomes natural after five years of observing the apes.
National Geographic Society

A blackback male, two females, and two juveniles cluster on a tree branch. Sitting in a tree fork, below, an infant gorilla clings to its mother's back.

G. B. Schaller,
Bruce Coleman, Inc.

Dian Fossey makes gorilla noseprints from close-up photographs.

Flossie is wide awake now, and hungry. Still lying down, she stretches out a long arm and pulls a nearby galium vine into her mouth. Then she sits up. She is a sloppy eater, and some of the leaves have spilled over onto her chest. Titus explores them with his mouth, then eats them. Gorilla mothers never feed their infants. It is by eating leftovers like this that Titus will gradually build up the same diet as his mother. Now, however, at the age of a year, what he really wants is milk, and as he picks away at the leaves, he finds Flossie's nipple, and curls up to have his breakfast.

Well fed and happy on this lovely morning, Titus takes advantage of the hagenia tree branches, where he has been sleeping, and climbs quickly to the top, about thirty feet above the ground. His long, spidery arms are ideal for tree-swinging, but only small animals actually spend much time in trees. The larger gorillas, especially the males, are too heavy to brachiate and know from experience that they may come crashing down as branches break beneath their weight. They are careful and only climb when special foods, like the purple fruit of the *Pygeum africanum,* come into season and tempt a whole gorilla group into one tree. Many large gorillas do not even build their sleeping nests in trees, but instead make an ersatz nest right on the ground.

Titus is still light, and at a year he thoroughly enjoys exploring the highest branches. But Flossie is impatient with him and barks short, staccato pants, a sound mother gorillas use to discipline their youngsters. Flossie knew what she was doing. A pitiful whine shatters the morning. Titus is stuck up in the tree. Although Flossie must hear his cries, she does not respond vocally. In fact, baby gorillas' cries usually go unanswered. But she does climb to the rescue, returning to the ground just as the silverback leader of the group, Uncle Bert, rises on all fours and signals by his stance that it is time to move. He is imposing, with his heavy torso resting on the knuckle pads that are like those of his cousin the chimpanzee. Because his arms are longer than his legs, his back slopes downward, giving him an impressive mien.

Uncle Bert is not the first silverback whom Fossey has known
to lead Group Four. When she first met them, an old male with
a throat impediment was in charge. He could only sound a rough,
horse-like vocalization, so Fossey dubbed him Whinny. Through
Whinny she habituated Group Four. Only after Whinny's death
did Uncle Bert become the Alpha male. At first he seemed un-
sure in his new role, and for a while the whole group, which had
once accepted Fossey easily, turned suspicious. Fossey deduced
from these newly turned cold shoulders that the attitude of the
silverback determined the personality of the group. Since then,
however, Uncle Bert has mellowed and Group Four has accepted her again into its midst.

Uncle Bert has surveyed the territory and made his decision.
He turns his head to the right and begins to move along the
ground toward the high grasses in the saddle area just below
him. Within minutes the group is gone.

The humans emerge from their hide to examine the gorillas'
nests, abandoned now. Gorillas, like chimps, do not use their
nests again, but instead seek shelter wherever they are at dusk.
For a long time no one realized that gorillas made nests at all.
They are usually crude platforms, only a vestige of the stronger
nests they needed when they were arboreal thousands of years
ago. Sitting on the ground at night, or in the low branches of a
tree, they pull down branches and twigs around themselves,
and sometimes add a cushion of moss and earth. They build up
a firm rim, like the sides of a youth bed, for a sense of security.

Although mature gorillas usually sleep alone, Fossey has observed an exception in Group Nine. When she first saw them,
this group included five males and one very old female she called
Koko. The five males all seemed to dote on Koko, and when she
became ill, Rafiki, the dominant silverback of Group Nine, took
to wandering through the forest with her. For several nights they
even shared a nest, until finally Rafiki returned to the group
alone. Koko had died. During her last days all the males treated
her as if she were an infant again. So perhaps this is not a real
exception; Rafiki sensed that Koko had become child-like and

so he took care of her as if she were a child, even to sleeping with her at night.

The nests that the observers now examine from Group Four are filled with dung. They take some samples and place them in containers in their haversacks to examine later. It should reveal what the gorillas have been eating and it may also divulge which parasites are living within their digestive tracts. Gorillas soil their nests, unlike the fastidious chimpanzees. But gorilla spoor is hard and rubbery, partially because the animals consume so little water, and it does not cling to their hair and dirty them. Gorillas do not worry about their excrement because they do not have to.

The forest is silent now, except for the intermittent call of birds. The absence of gorilla noises reminds the observers that they should hurry to catch up with the group. Their trail is easy to follow. Broken branches and more spoor lead directly to the animals. Even before they can see them again, the humans can hear the "pig grunts," a sound Fossey describes as a crowd of pigs meeting at a trough. Every animal in the group grunts as they move along, possibly as a way of keeping together when they cannot see each other through the thick undergrowth. These grunts, barks, and *wraaghs* provide a warning system, and may also herald the discovery of good forage.

The saddle area is rich in towering grasses and clusters of tiny yellow and white flowers. Suddenly the humans spot Titus, riding higher than the grasses on his mother's back. He is holding on tight to her hairs as Flossie bends to munch some wild celery. It was in one of these celery patches that Fossey first won a gorilla's trust by breaking off a stalk and pretending to eat it as if she were enjoying the most delicious treat. Fossey has never seen the gorillas drinking water in the wild and assumes that they get what they need from the juicy celery, bamboo, and occasional fruits and flowers they consume. The humans crouch in a comfortable position. They will watch the gorillas foraging for at least an hour. The amount of time the apes spend filling up their stomachs varies, depending on the season and the amount of rain that has just fallen.

While they eat, the gorillas emit another sound, *naoom, naoom, naoom!* It is a sound Fossey is skilled at imitating. She has even crept, unseen, into their midst when they were eating and begun to make this *naoom* herself, setting off a chain of responses from the whole assemblage of gorillas, which proved not only her talent as an animal impersonator, but the fact that this sound elicits rejoinders from the group. She has also belched *naoom* openly to win acceptance from the animals. It seems to mean that the food is plentiful and tasty.

Uncle Bert is finished eating and leads his group through a field of nettles as he heads toward another slope. The humans feel the stinging plants as they push through with their gloved hands. One false step, and a nettle swings back, whipping the newcomer across the cheek, mercifully missing his eye. The pain is sharp and constant, but this is no place to stop. The observers move on, and soon they are on a ridge where the undergrowth is thick beneath the pleasant shadow of the vernonia tree.

As they pass by they notice the tracks of duiker and buffalo, who have kept this trail clear of undergrowth. One of the humans stops suddenly, pointing to the body of a freshly killed duiker. The gorillas must have just passed it too, but not one of them even stopped to sniff. Gorillas in the wild do not seem interested in meat, even if it is there, ready-killed for them. In captivity gorillas are as delighted with a meat dinner as any chimpanzee, who in the wild has been seen to actively hunt it. Gorillas seem to have an innate taste for meat, but nothing in their mountain environment has ever led them to sample it.

In fact, gorillas are mainly herbivorous (plant eaters). Along with their favored vernonia tree, they eat vines and fungus, but ignore eggs even when the birds have deserted their nests. The only animal food gorillas eat are the juicy slugs that they suck out of the insides of rotting trees, and the small gray snails that cling to the undersides of the nettle leaves.

Uncle Bert is still moving, apparently not satisfied with this particular vernonia tree. The humans keep their distance, for they have not yet revealed themselves. Suddenly, Uncle Bert emits a *wraagh!* that sets the hair on end of the observer whose face is still smarting from the nettle. The gorillas disperse. Only now do the observers move closer to see what happened.

Uncle Bert almost collided with a herd of buffalo whose presence was obscured by the foliage. But they were more scared than he—gorillas have no real predators except for an occasional leopard, and man. The buffalo back off.

All is quiet on the slope until a small cry captures Uncle Bert's attention. It is Titus again. Flossie had dashed off in alarm and left her baby behind. Titus's cries increase; he works himself up into a full-scale temper tantrum before Flossie returns and holds him to her breast. Titus sucks away and Flossie hurries off to catch up with the group, moving on three limbs now, for she is clutching Titus to her breast with the fourth.

Gradually the group reassembles near another tree. Uncle Bert has selected a sunny spot for their afternoon rest. The gorillas are taking advantage of this respite from the wind and rain and stretch out to enjoy a long siesta. When the sun appears after weeks of rain, they may spend as many as five hours literally soaking up sunshine.

A young blackback drops down first, sprawled on the damp earth. But Uncle Bert approaches him; he has apparently decided that this is the very spot he wanted to lie down on. He nudges the younger animal, who indicates his submission to the silverback by bending over and turning his rump toward him in the familiar ape posture. Then he crawls away to find another spot farther down the slope.

Uncle Bert leans over from where he is sitting and pulls some foliage up around him. The observers watch him make his day nest, a skimpy version of the one he climbed out of earlier that morning. Scattered around him are the rest of Group Four— Flossie with Titus beside her, and little Cleo. Most of them have not bothered making nests but are just sprawled in the sunlight.

Afternoon

While the adult gorillas doze, the humans whisper to each other. They avoid speaking aloud, for they know from experience that human voices alarm the animals. Should they drift apart, they whistle. After a while one of the humans feels like stretching his legs, and thinking that all the grown animals are asleep, he moves across an open space. But Uncle Bert spots him, and rises upright on two legs. Angry, Uncle Bert breaks branches all around him and begins loud barking. Then he releases a heavy odor into the air, and stops. Fossey describes this kind of display as "mild alarm." Uncle Bert is calm now that the human has crouched down again and is not threatening him. Still uneasy, however, Uncle Bert sticks a piece of straw into his mouth and sucks on it, looking very much like a human who bites down on a pipe when nervous.

After a while Uncle Bert lies down again and the infants and juveniles begin to play. While Fossey was habituating the animals to her presence, play was the one activity that her presence in-hibited most. Now that they are used to her, the youngsters have resumed their normal rough-and-tumble wrestling bouts, and their sometimes reckless explorations of their own physical skills, literally going out on a limb, all the while getting to know each other and the world around them. Fossey estimates that these youngsters spend half their time at play.

Play is a familiar word, but it becomes complicated when different people try to define it. One way of looking at play is how it lets young primates, including young humans, imitate in frag-mented and exaggerated ways the many actions of their elders with a particular goal in mind. For example, gorilla youngsters play at nest-building in order to learn how to do it when they are older. They also play at child-care, so that they will be skilled at this when the time comes. Play also gives young animals a chance to develop their muscles, so they chase each other, climb trees, swing from branch to branch, and wrestle. Finally, in play-ing with other animals, both their peers and older members of the group, they learn how to get along in the hierarchy.

Gorillas, like other primates, first play alone. Titus, who is still very small, enjoys sliding down his mother's back. Cleo has discovered that Uncle Bert's great silver back is better, and she has used him for a slide. She also likes to slide down tree trunks and twisting vines. Sliding is just about the favorite play of small gorillas.

The observers are enjoying the antics of the young apes. One little male is placing clods of moss upon his head and walking around bipedally, apparently looking for a laugh. Cleo approaches and tickles him, and he drops the clod and falls to the ground, wrestling with her. All the while the two are frolicking, they emit soft chuckling sounds and let their mouths fall open in a relaxed, friendly gorilla version of a grin.

Groups seldom have many infants the same age. One year Fossey only recorded two births among the animals she was observing. So most play has to be between juveniles and infants, or even between juveniles and adults. Female juveniles especially are interested in the infants and often borrow one for a while to play "Auntie" with.

Almost as often, however, the small animals seek out large adult males. It is wonderful to see these large animals control their strength in order to play gently with the littler ones. Fossey herself once encountered a young blackback in a tree. When he demanded, vocally, that she give him the right of way, she refused for fear of falling. Then the animal pressed down on her shoulders in the same way he would press down on another gorilla. Fossey discovered that he exerted very slight pressure. He could have hurt her, but he restrained his strength in the same way that the grown animals control themselves when they play with the small ones.

Although the gorilla family is made up of mother and child, the males tolerate all the playful youngsters and are concerned when trouble arrives. Fossey watched one day as a small juvenile played around and on top of Uncle Bert. She was afraid that the sometimes crotchety old silverback would grow angry with the smaller gorilla. But when he finally did react, he had a long-stemmed flower in his hand and used it to tickle the delighted youngster. Silverbacks often carry around small animals for days at a time, and frightened infants have been found beside the corpses of murdered silverbacks. Although the male gorilla cannot know which children are his, he is appealingly solicitous of all those in his group.

Gorilla mothers may not object when an adolescent female or adult male borrows her juvenile, but they are very protective when their babies are tiny. One perplexed mother carried the corpse of her infant for days, not wanting to give it up, not comprehending death. Although gorillas can cling, unaided, when they are born, the mother usually gives a hand to her baby anyway. Fossey has watched a new mother climb as high as eighty feet into a tree top for food, her day-old infant clinging precariously to her stomach hairs. The mother crawled out on a limb, as the infant slid down. The observer, on the ground, was prepared to catch the falling infant. The tiny one continued slipping until it reached its mother's ankles. Only then did she seem to notice and pushed it back up to her chest again. Perhaps this kind of adventure gives the youngsters their taste for heights.

Climbing and tumbling monopolizes their play, but infant apes also like to explore. Curious about everything, the young animals invade the humans' gear, examining their equipment and whatever they can find inside the haversack—pencils, spiral notebooks, containers, anything.

Curiosity seems to diminish with age, or perhaps with the arrival of responsibility. After the five bachelors in Group Nine had lost their beloved Koko, Fossey remarked that they acted more happy-go-lucky than the other gorillas. Free from females and infants, they were more concerned with everything around them, including herself.

Titus and Cleo are still playing. They have scarcely paused all afternoon. But now the adults are awake and for them the rest of this midafternoon break means time for grooming. All nonhuman primates groom their hair as a form of hygiene, and all of the great apes, in some manner, also use grooming as a way to socialize. But most of the gorilla grooming is done by themselves. They part their own hair with their fingers and pick out small insects or flecks of dry skin with their hands and mouths. They only present a part of their body to another animal to groom when they are not able to reach it themselves.

Infants do not groom at all, for their mothers take care of them. Occasionally, however, a gorilla will groom another gorilla to socialize. When Koko was alive, she would begin to groom one of the males in Group Nine and set off a whole chain of grooming, the six animals lined up grooming one another. After her death, the five remaining males stopped grooming altogether. Fossey does not yet fully understand the place of grooming in gorilla behavior.

The long midday break can also be a time for mating. But gorillas do not seem as constantly interested as the chimpanzees. Females show no visible sign of estrus, but are ready to receive a male once a month for several days.

A lone male has made his way into the resting area. He is familiar to the observers, and the other animals seem to recognize him too as an outcast who used to belong to the group. They do not respond in any way to his arrival. But he senses that the childless female is in estrus and he approaches her. He begins shaking branches and making brief dashes through the under- brush, all for her benefit. All the time he is courting her, Uncle Bert is only a few feet away. Now the loner approaches and mates with her from the rear, right next to the silverback. Uncle Bert does not seem to care very much. The Alpha male is not possessive about the females in his group. Sexual activity is ap- parently less frequent among gorillas than among other primates. The animals do not appear to resent a visitor as long as that visitor is familiar and does not try to take the female away.

But there is some competition for females. Some lone male silverbacks who have either left a group freely or been pushed out try to start groups of their own. They do this by a display of force, and kidnap females, some along with their infants. Fossey is now studying the whole system of how groups form and re- form.

The gorillas are restless as Uncle Bert leads Group Four down from the ridge in search of their afternoon meal. He does not backtrack, but seeks a fresh, ungrazed area. He wanders into a grove of hagenia trees where he discovers some of their favorite foods growing. Large and brown, looking like a Frisbee but smelling like raw mushrooms, is a bracket fungus. It takes dozens of years for just one to grow, and it is a favorite gorilla food.

They have only begun to eat when another gorilla group appears. The observers drop back behind the safety of another tree trunk, ready for trouble. The new group is smaller than Uncle Bert's, but it has three silverbacks and two blackbacks in it. The lieutenants in both groups, however, retire to the sidelines. They let their leaders take over.

Uncle Bert rises bipedally. At his full height the humans can see that he towers over them. Cupping his great hands, he raps out a hollow, bullet-popping, rhythmic beat on his chest. Intermittently, he whacks the foliage and thumps the ground. As he moves, he repeats a whole series of echoing *hoo* sounds, as many as eighty-four times, faster and faster, until suddenly he breaks this rhythm and rushes forward, mouth open, lips drawn back in a grimace that is meant to frighten away most other creatures. It usually does just that. The entire "display"—chest-beating, ground-thumping, and total devastation of the foliage within his reach—is usually a bluff, a way to release tension and disconcert an enemy. A great silverback once threatened Fossey this way, finally rushing at her. But she stood her ground and held out her arms, crying *whoaah!,* and the gorilla stopped short. Gorillas who have been attacked by hunters have been known to bite. However, they have not been known to make the first move.

Displays like Uncle Bert's are often matched by parallel actions from the opposing silverback. But today the two Alpha males are actually fighting, swatting at each other with powerful hands, really injuring each other. Flossie, who has been watching from the side, is starting to emit quick, soft expulsions of air, almost whisper-soft, in what Fossey calls a pant series. She is caught up in the battle and seems to be cheering as spectators in a stadium chant support of the home team.

The encounter ends with the intruders moving off. When they are less than a mile away, their silverback emits a *hoo,* and

Uncle Bert responds. They have established a safe working distance between them. Encounters like this occur often, but usually the threat display is sufficient and they avoid physical contact. Tragedy has occurred, however, when the silverback happened to be carrying an infant during a confrontation. The infants have died, victims of battle.

Alone again, the members of Group Four continue to eat the bracket fungus until they follow Uncle Bert down into another patch of nettles. The observers are watching from a distance when they hear a loud *wraagh!* They look up and glimpse a Tutsi hunter running away. Gorillas are especially wary of the Africans .who have hunted them for so long and flee when they see them. Fossey's African trackers are familiar to the apes, but they seldom come close to each other.

It is growing late and the observers separate. Each has a job waiting back at camp. A thunderclap, and the remaining human unpacks the nylon raincoat he has been carrying all day. Another crack seems to fracture the still air, freezing him in place.

Uncle Bert is startled too. He roars. Then, as rain pours down on the lush meadow, Uncle Bert charges the storm, beating his chest and slashing at the branches in his rage. But the rain pounds down harder. The observer can barely see through to where Uncle Bert is still standing, ten yards away. Up on his back legs, the silverback looks as if he is trying to make his body surface smaller, as if he hates his hands and chest to get wet. Gorillas seem unhappy in the rain, yet they endure it without seeking shelter. Ironically, gorillas who live in the rain forest find water, in general, uncomfortable. When the group reaches the narrow stream that flows across the meadow, they step across it, never letting their feet submerge.

The sudden storm has hastened the end of daylight. With evening upon them, the gorillas move into the arms of a low hypericum tree and begin making nests. Gorillas are diurnal like the chimpanzees, and ourselves; their waking hours follow the sun.

Across the meadow the observer sees camp; the small cabins

washed by the rain are glistening as he heads toward them. The rain has already moved on. Suddenly he hears a whistle, his signal, and he whistles back, then waits. He hears the signal again, and this time the whistler comes into view—a small bird, a regular afternoon caller.

Nearby, another bird, nearly a foot tall, is sitting on a branch, its blue feathers turning purple as the sun goes down. The observer hurries on. The pit fire is glowing in the camp, matching the flaming sunset beyond the trees.

PART III

ORANGUTANS

Biruté Galdikas at her camp in Borneo with two infant orangutan rehabilitants.

7

Biruté Galdikas in Borneo

Halfway around the world from Central Africa, no moonlight slips through the leafy canopy that rises eighty feet above the Indonesian rain forest. Before dawn breaks, filling the air with green-filtered light, Biruté Galdikas-Brindamour is awake on the stilted platform she calls Camp Dart. This is one of three stations she and her husband, Rod Brindamour, have built among the trees in the Tanjung Puting Nature Reserve on the island of Borneo. Alert, listening to the morning cry of a red leaf-eating monkeys, Galdikas and Brindamour slip from their rope hammocks down to the sweltering forest floor. They hurry to where they watched Nick, a large male orangutan, build his nest twelve hours earlier, and arrive in time to see Nick stretch his long, hairy arms, copper in the early sunlight. Nick ignores them. He is habituated to these humans who have followed him continuously now for forty-five days.

Biruté and Rod Brindamour were both twenty-five years old in November of 1971 when they arrived on this island in the Java Sea, part of the Indonesian archipelago. Galdikas had already completed most of her graduate studies at UCLA with Louis Leakey as her adviser. She had just visited Gombe and had the example of Goodall and her camp to guide her. And she is the only one of Leakey's trio of "ape girls" to work as part of a team. From the beginning, the orangutan project has been a joint effort.

When Leakey met the young man whom Galdikas introduced as her fiancé, Leakey suggested that Rod Brindamour interrupt his physics studies and go along to Indonesia. Leakey was impressed by Brindamour's knowledge of his native Canadian woods, as well as his technical skills. He was the obvious candidate for project photographer and administrator. Leakey also saw a practical advantage to Brindamour's presence. He sensed that the Indonesian authorities might be more sympathetic to a man, especially an experienced forester, than to a young woman on her own.

At thirty years of age, Galdikas's wide-spaced gray eyes still reflect a sense of wonder, like a schoolgirl's. In the field she wears blue jeans and shirt, and tucks her long brown hair into a flat khaki hat. She is slim and wiry, like her husband, of the same medium height, and she shares with him an aura of confidence built upon their joint success.

Galdikas is where she has always dreamed of being, in a remote setting, ready for adventure. She was a traveler before she could talk; her Lithuanian parents had stopped temporarily in Wiesbaden, Germany, where she was born in 1946, on their way to refuge in North America. The Galdikas family settled in Toronto, Canada, and there, in the public library, their eldest daughter found the books that fed her passion for far-flung places. Later, when the family moved to California, she studied psychology, zoology, and anthropology at UCLA. Her first field work took place during a summer project in the distant hills of Yugoslavia, examining Neolithic caves. Back in California, she pushed farther back in time, investigating aboriginal sites.

Like Leakey himself, Biruté Galdikas became interested in primates through her curiosity about human evolution. Eventually she focused on the least understood, most elusive of all the Pongidae—the orangutan.

It took two years to raise money for her project. While she waited, she spent hundreds of hours watching six captive orangs at the Los Angeles Zoo. Before the zoo's new facilities were ready, the apes lived in small concrete cages. All they did was sit listlessly and wait for food. It made her wonder all the more what their native habitat was like. Was it captivity, or something about the Indonesian islands of Sumatra and Borneo that had led these highly intelligent apes to become such lethargic creatures?

Since her arrival on Borneo in 1971, Galdikas has begun to find the answer. Here rainfall varies from drizzle to downpour the year round. There are clear days during the short dry season, but on the average the humidity is 98 percent, and the temperature is a steady 90° F. Over five hundred different trees bloom erratically. A few fruit in alternate years, some less frequently, while others may produce a crop two or three times a season. Lean months follow lush ones without any discernible pattern. And the great male orangutans, like Nick, sound their eerie long-calls several times a day. In the first year, the Brindamours did not understand the meaning of these cries.

Until recently Borneo was infamous as the land of Dyak headhunters, and the king cobra. But the Dyaks have changed their diet, and the cobra does not inhabit Kalimantan Province. Even so, the forests are at least as inhospitable to scientists as the African mountain woodland. Flat and at sea level, most of the thirty-five acres of her study area is primary forest, filled with *meranti* and *ramen* trees, that has not changed for millions of years. A small part is swamp, broken by the tributaries of the Sekonyer Kanan River that flows less than two miles from base camp. The remaining area is *ladang,* overgrown fields slashed and burned by nomadic dry-rice farmers. The ladang is treacherous—sun-hungry undergrowth gone wild struggling for space. Untended for less than a year, *alang-alang* grass devastates fields and huts, totally submerging everything in high, tangled vines.

Indonesian families live in small villages nearby, where they fish, farm, hunt, and sometimes work tapping latex palms for rubber companies, or cutting down the other precious trees. Villagers speak Malay, a language that has no words for gender but simply calls a child a child and all humans, people. Long ago they called the strange, shaggy, red-haired ape the *orang hutan,* the "wild person of the woods."

Galdikas is comfortable among these people. They like her

too, and are pleased that she has sought Indonesian citizenship. She plans to stay among the orangutan for a long time.

The Indonesians have lived near the apes for centuries. Charred orang bones found across the island in the Niah Caves show that thousands of years ago their distant ancestors hunted apes for food. They have eaten the orangs, built legends around them, and kept them as pets in pretty collars and chains. That is illegal now that the orangutan has been designated an endangered species (optimists estimate that about three thousand still range freely). Black marketeers still kidnap infants and trade them for transistor radios or watches. Then the traded animals are sold for thousands of dollars to unscrupulous zoos or circuses.

Orangutans in the wild had only been studied by a handful of scientists, including an Englishman, John MacKinnon, and an American, Peter Rodman, before Galdikas began her work. They had spent stretches of several months at a time over a period of years observing the general pattern of orangutan behavior and the total ecology of the rain forests. What they reported about orangutan adaptation was that these apes were solitary, mainly arboreal, and ate fruit. The ape's lethargy, combined with the miserable climate, defeated more prolonged research.

Borneo is harder to endure than Central Africa. The damp is unrelenting; there is no respite from the heat or the monotonous shrieking of tropical birds and the cacophony of the gibbons. When the Brindamours arrived in November 1971, they built one base, Camp Leakey. The Indonesian family on their staff helped them raise a traditional forest hut on stilts with open sides and low-hanging thatched eaves to keep out the rain. On a kerosene stove they cooked dull meals of canned sardines, bananas, and rice. From Camp Leakey they hacked away a hundred and fifty miles of crisscrossing trails with their machetes as they slowly mapped the Reserve.

The first year passed painfully. They watched their clothing rot off their backs, their leather shoes decay from damp. Brindamour saw funguses erupt inside his cameras and rust ruin his tape recorder. During the rainiest season the swamp waters rose, and they found some tributary pools dark with crocodiles. As they waded waist high through streams, inch-long leeches latched onto their legs and thighs. And when they were pulled off, more attached themselves, and they played a nightmarish game of leapfrog with the bloodsuckers.

After a particularly heavy rain red ants swarmed out of their hills hungry for flesh. And all the while tropical ulcers bloomed on their arms and legs. Then, insidiously, malaria—the occupational hazard of the tropics—struck.

Overwhelmed at times, the Brindamours kept their spirits up by conjuring mirages of ice cream stands among the palms and listening through static to "Voice of America" breakfast shows on their shortwave radio. At first they devoured outdated magazines and wrote letters home demanding news—news of the world, their families, any detail of the life they had left behind.

Slowly, however, they began to forget about the radio, junk food, and word from abroad, as they defeated the nuisances that plagued them. Brindamour discovered that salt chased leeches, that a controlled kerosene fire ended ant attacks. Better medicine controls their malaria now, and antibiotics cure the ulcers.

As Galdikas's eyes grew familiar with the forest, events inside that magic world grew more important than news of far-off wars and demonstrations. She wrote home for nylon clothing, and styrofoam and polyester casings for their equipment. They planted a garden of tropical fruits, and became delighted with a wild civet who began to pay regular visits to their kitchen hut each evening. Soon the gibbons' calls and the atonal, staccato rasping of the tropical birds turned into music.

All the while Galdikas was slowly, very slowly, habituating the wild orangutan. At first they seemed too easy to contact. She had been prepared to search for months, but she saw some the very day she arrived. High in the ramen trees, they noticed her, and just climbed higher as she watched through her binoculars. She believed then, as the earlier primatologists had reported, that orangutans are completely arboreal.

Despite the chronic misery, she began a census of the apes and a catalog of the two hundred different kinds of foods they eat. She began to recognize individuals by their faces and by their calls. And soon she named them for their looks, or on a whim, because they reminded her of someone she had known or read about.

Orangutan faces look more human than the African apes. They have high, smooth foreheads without great overhanging brows or the sagittal crest. Their eyes are rounder and set closer together, and their small ears are disconcertingly like our own. Long, shaggy red hair covers their bodies. Their arms and legs are longer in proportion to their bodies than the African apes. And they do not have knuckle pads to cushion their four-legged walk.

Even more striking, however, is the sexual dimorphism, the enormous physical differences between the males and females. The female orangs grow to be about three and a half feet tall, and weigh on the average seventy pounds. But the males grow a foot and a half taller and weigh as much as one hundred and fifty pounds. As the male orangutan matures, he begins to grow thick pads of flesh that frame his face, cheek pads, and a great pouch develops at his throat, which he inflates when he wants to sound his long-call. Some zoologists think these differences are enough to put them into a different genus. They call the African apes *Pan,* and the orangutan *Pongo*.

Although gorillas are sexually dimorphic too, they are not quite as much. More than physical differences distinguish the orangs from the other great apes. They behave differently. Their social life is meager, with the giant adult males spending most of their days alone. Wary of humans, they stayed aloft when Galdikas began to track them, revealing their anger at her intrusion by smacking their lips and tossing branches down at her.

Gradually she got to know them, and they her. The Brindamours discovered they could recognize the long-call of an individual ape as clearly as his face. Today they know at least forty-nine orangutans by name and personality, and she has begun to chart family histories for many of them.

George Buctel

Tanjung Puting Nature Reserve in Borneo

After a while Galdikas established a routine. She spent roughly
two weeks at a stretch in the forest following orangutans. The
rest of the month she stayed at Camp Leakey, analyzing her results. She would set out with her husband, a styrofoam box on his
back packed with notepaper, cameras, food, medicine, and surgical tools.

Galdikas made her first breakthrough one day in 1972 when,
after accidentally slashing her leg with a machete, she was taking
the shortest way back to camp through the ladang. Dripping
with blood, she stopped short on the narrow path. In the high
grass thirty feet from her, and at least a hundred yards from any
trees on either side, a subadult male orangutan was walking on
all fours. She marveled to see him on the ground so far from the

forest. It showed her that orangutans are in part terrestrial and that they were still not revealing themselves completely to her.

Today Galdikas has habituated several adult males who spend at least 17 percent of their day on the ground and do as much as 100 percent of their traveling on foot. With two auxiliary camps now, Camp Wilkie and Camp Dart, the Brindamours can sleep in the tracking area when they are far from base camp.

Leaving Camp Leakey, she takes one of the many paths into the forest. Walking here is easier, for in this rare wilderness where man has never felled the trees, the sun is caught in the leaves of the canopy, and the soil below is rich and free from tangled undergrowth.

When her sensitive ears pick up the thud of falling fruit skins, she knows that an orangutan is feeding somewhere nearby. She finds the animal with her binoculars and may recognize Nick, the adult male she has known since 1973. He appeared in the reserve suddenly after the first mature male she had been tracking, T.P. (so named because his throat pouch never deflated), suddenly disappeared. Nick holds a special place for Galdikas, for he is the wild orangutan she has followed for the longest time.

As she walks, her concentration is total. She used to be a daydreamer, but now she is constantly attuned to the present. She watches Nick, but she is also on the lookout for cobras and pythons, which she does not want to startle into an offensive attack. Nothing is casual. Each move is careful, even when she rests. Soon after her arrival in Borneo, she sat down exhausted on a dead log, only to leap up in pain! But what had felt just like an insect bite, she soon discovered, was the log itself, exuding an acidic sap that burned her.

She tries to stay with her husband, but if they are tracking a pair of animals which separate, they diverge too, each taking one orangutan. They always carry compasses, since it is easy to get lost in the forest. Alone, they have to depend on whistles to keep in touch, because walkie-talkies are useless in dense jungle. They reunite at Camp Dart. Night falls abruptly here at the equator. They are usually very tired from twelve hours in the field, but before they drift off to sleep, Biruté and Rod Brinda-mour recapitulate their adventures and observations, comparing everything.

Both of them are totally immersed in the research. Their life together is very much as life must have been on the frontier a hundred years ago in North America. Each couple is its own center of gravity, and survival takes up a great part of each day. But whereas the frontier families had many interests, the Brinda-mours have only one—the orangutan. They use each other to test out theories, to puzzle over the idiosyncrasies of these highly individual animals.

And when Biruté Galdikas falls asleep at night, Nick and T.P. and the other orangutans invade her dreams. When she wakes up, she almost remembers what the orangs revealed, and then it all slips away, although she tries to hang on to the thread. Wide awake, she lets it go and rises in the dark to begin another day of patient tracking.

8

Camp Leakey

Camp Leakey has grown since 1971, not as Gombe grew, but in a different way. It is much more comfortable now because an electric generator, a water pump, and a refrigerator have moderated the worst aspects of the tropical climate. But the biggest changes have been within the population of the camp—the orangutan population. For while the Tanjung Puting Reserve has been operating as a scientific field station, at the same time Galdikas has been directing a rehabilitation center for young confiscated orangutans in cooperation with the Indonesian department of forestries, trying to rehabilitate the orphaned youngsters to life in the wild.

She calls them rehabs, the half-dozen orangutans in Camp Leakey at any one time which dominate the scene. The first one, Sugito, arrived in 1971, shortly after they had settled into the rain forest. The authorities had confiscated Sugito from poachers who had probably killed his mother before jamming him into a small wooden crate. Only a few months old, he was in awful shape, but he responded to Galdikas immediately, adopting her as his "stepmother." Sugito clung to her night and day, as a wild-born orang clings to its ape mother for at least the first eighteen months of life.

Soon after Sugito, two more infants arrived, and Galdikas discovered that each small ape behaved quite differently from the others. While Sugito whined and cried for four whole days when Galdikas had gone to Kumai, thirty miles away by river, in a narrow dugout, a small female slept happily in her washbasin-crib, clinging to mosquito netting.

Rehabilitating small apes to the wild was not one of the things Galdikas had learned in graduate school. There were no precedents to follow. Some people doubted it could be done at all. But Galdikas is concerned about the rapidly dwindling wild population and decided to try. She planned to give them as much freedom as possible, and at the same time teach them about the forest as soon as they could cling comfortably to the low branches.

Leading the small animals into the trees, she helps them feel at home there and tries to show them the kinds of foods their wild mothers ate. By July 1972, four of the rehabs had returned to the wild, two with apparent success, for they disappeared completely, while the other two remained nearby, but returned to camp less often as the months went by.

But other rehabs, like Sugito, remain with her. He has been joined by other confiscated youngsters, some of which had lived as pets with Indonesian families and are extraordinarily skilled at imitating human behavior.

The Brindamours had built small closed huts for their supplies, but they still slept in their forest hut, high on stilts with open sides to let the breezes through. The heavy forest foliage provided privacy from other humans. But the small rehabs climbed up into their home as if it were another tree. Once there, they delighted in all the artifacts of human life. The mattresses and bedclothes offered them a seemingly endless source of rolling, bouncing, and tumbling space. They ransacked supplies, toppling containers, dumping baskets, and when not constantly watched, produced general mayhem among photographic supplies and carefully accumulated scientific data.

The clever infants used doorknobs to open closed doors, effortlessly opened "toddler-proof" medicine bottles, and poked their heads up through the thatched roof to inspect the weather. Seeing was not enough for them. The small orangs tasted everything too. Arriving back in camp after a two-week stint in the forest, the Brindamours once found that a newly liberated rehab had come back to look for them, and not seeing her step-mother, had climbed inside their bed to wait, and meanwhile chewed a favorite old cocoa can, leaving her tooth marks as evidence of her visit.

The older juvenile rehabs invade everything, while the younger ones cling tightly to Galdikas constantly, making an art of the once simple chore of changing clothes.

The mischievousness of the small orangutans in camp is a mind-boggling paradox in contrast to the sobriety of the solitary orangutans in the wild. Living with humans, the rehabs parody human behavior, which is the very antithesis of the way they be-have in the wild. At camp they are social and hang around to-gether, seemingly concocting trouble. They apparently enjoy each other as well as other animals. Sugito has spent countless hours cuddling, cooing to, and even kissing the small pet cat which is part of the Brindamour household. Kissing the cat, Sugito puckers up his lips, displaying one of a series of facial expressions that are seldom seen on wild orangs which, except in moments of distress, seem to keep a dead pan much of the time.

Most bewildering of all is the rehabs' use of tools. No one has ever seen wild orangs use anything but their hands to dig in-sects out of the ground. But the rehabs watch humans and delight in working the water pump, using their agile feet as another pair of hands. They have no trouble getting a drink of water. When the young female, Cempaka, who had lived for seven years with an Indonesian family, arrived at camp, she ate her rice with a spoon as the family did, and sometimes Sugito joined her, eat-ing with a spoon daintily from his bowl. Cempaka even made herself a tool by breaking a stick in half and using it to dig with. And if the mood struck her, she could crack an egg into a bowl and go through the motions of stirring pancake batter.

The rehabs combine their playful imitations of humans with instincts that are pure orangutan. Sugito, for instance, adores putting things on his head, the way the wild orangs build plat-forms to protect themselves from rain. He, who never watched an ape mother cover her head, nonetheless draped burlap around his own, or sometimes borrowed his stepmother's khaki hat,

and even placed the docile kitten on his head—for a short time—
as if to say, "Remember, I'm still an ape."

Suppertime at Camp Leakey can be frustrating for Galdikas.
With the newest infant recruit clinging to her shoulders, the
larger rehabs like Sugito hovering around, she scarcely gets a
fraction of her food into her mouth before an orang swipes it.
When Sugito grabbed her last bite one evening, she muttered
to him as if he were a child, "But that's not fair!" Her husband,
unharassed by the orangutans, looked up then from his empty
plate, advising her to "learn to eat a little faster!"

Brindamour is right, of course. No matter how clever the
small orangutans are at caricaturing their human friends, they
do not respond to discipline. Galdikas could not house-train them
or teach them table manners to accompany their dexterity with
a spoon and fork.

Unlike the African apes, whose mothers discipline them in
order to teach them the codes of their species, orang mothers
never admonish their children. There is no reason to. They have
no social codes because, as an adult, the wild orangutan avoids
other members of its species most of the time and does not have
a "social" life like the African apes.

The rehabs cannot learn discipline in camp. Yet despite her
efforts to teach them to be wild again, they do become socialized,
especially those which stay a long time. When the socialized
apes leave for the forest, many of them cluster together near
Camp Leakey. They depend on each other in a most unorangu-
tan-like way.

Galdikas finds it hard to break the ties between herself and a
rehab like Sugito. She learned the technique she is perfecting
by watching a wild orangutan mother force her small son out of
her nest when a new baby arrived. The wild mother literally
pushed him out and was very mean to him, so mean that he began
to whimper when she even looked his way. The mother softened
her dismissal, however, by wrestling with him playfully as she
had never done before. He got the message, and soon began
nesting and then traveling on his own.

As Camp Leakey grew more crowded, and the former rehabs

haunted the nearby forest, the Brindamours made several significant changes in the way they lived. First they built a wooden, white-painted, screen-windowed, almost totally orangutan-proof house. At last they had a respite from their charges.

Next they built a feeding station, a "halfway" house two hundred and fifty feet from camp, where the animals could make a gradual transition from camp life to the wild. The orang feeding station, unlike Goodall's banana boxes at Gombe, is for rehabs only. Galdikas does not feed the wild orangutans for fear of altering their natural behavior. But she does provide for the rehabs and she worries about them. She is afraid that they may not be able to compete for fruits and insects with their wild-bred relatives.

At the feeding station, which is a large, elevated wooden platform with scaffolding for the apes to swing from, she brings them food, but not too much. She hopes not only to divert their appetites from her own table, but to encourage them to supplement their diet with wild vegetation. The halfway house is really a place for them to learn slowly about life inside the forest. Sugito has already given up his burlap sack and builds a nest in trees nearby at night. If Sugito can make it, so can the rest.

The crucial test for the rehabs will come after they mature. Then Galdikas will see if they can compete for mates, as well as food, with the free-ranging animals. Camp living has made them look different from the wild animals she has gotten to know. Even without bars and chains, they look like captives, well-cared-for zoo apes which are larger, their red hair shinier, and altogether healthier than free-ranging animals. In zoos orangutan males often grow twice as large as wild apes, as heavy as three hundred pounds. And zoo females have their babies at an earlier age and more often than wild mothers.

If the rehabs are successful in the wild, and if they can reproduce, will these playful, tool-using animals remember their camp experiences? And if they do, will they pass it on to another generation? These are curious possibilities that the Brindamours are eager to observe as their project lengthens.

Meanwhile, because they are there in camp, Galdikas studies

them. She uses the rehabilitants as a resource, the way Fossey studied the orphaned gorilla babies she nursed to health in Rwanda. Galdikas keeps records on each animal, weighing them regularly on a wooden swing anchored to a tree that lends an air of suburbia to Camp Leakey. But the swing is not a toy, for rigged into the branches are a set of weights. When Galdikas sits down, she takes an infant orang on her lap and Brindamour weighs them together, then subtracts his wife's weight from the total.

Like a good stepmother, she takes her charges for a blood test periodically, holding out their arms for Brindamour to find a vein. Although orangs are not as close to humans physiologically as chimps, they are close enough to suffer the same diseases, from colds to malaria. Galdikas may eventually be able to study hormone changes in the orangutan, for she is convinced that this must account for the radical personality differences between females and males, and between the young animals and the grown ones.

Galdikas regards Sugito. He was at first so reluctant to leave the camp for the feeding station that she had to half drag him along the narrow dirt path into the trees. Soon he will develop a throat pouch, cheek flaps, and perhaps a beard that will turn her playful imp into a jowly-looking old man. When that happens, Galdikas knows she will feel a certain sadness. She is especially fond of him, and grateful too. She is convinced that the wild orangutans, the real subjects of her work, accepted her presence more easily when they saw him on her shoulder, probably taking her for some strange albino female ape.

Breaking the ties with the older rehabs is easier now. At Camp Leakey two biology students from Djakarta now help, as well as the Indonesian women on her staff. The field days have expanded from two-week absences from Camp Leakey to sometimes forty or fifty days at a time, as she and her husband follow a wild orangutan for as long as they can keep it in sight. The separations from the rehabs have grown so long that those animals who are able to live alone give up. Orphaned again, they take to the tree tops, wild once more.

9

The Wild Orangutans

Morning

Dawn is a lazy time at the top of the broad-leafed ramen palms. Although the human observers had to force themselves awake in dim darkness, the orangutans are barely stirring as the sky brightens over their sturdy tree nests. The taste of coffee still fresh in their mouths, the humans watch Georgina, a young mother with her first infant, Gale. Georgina sits up and peers over the edge of her nest, sixty feet down to the forest floor. Then she lies back and stares up another hundred feet to the interlocking branches that form a canopy over the forest.

Below, the humans shift restlessly and focus binoculars on Georgina, catching by chance a glimpse of a rainbow-colored bird preening itself on a higher branch. The humans listen to the drone of wild bees, the *rat-a-tat* of tropical birds and, always a joy, the lilting song of a gibbon. A large butterfly floats down between them, its brilliant colors shimmering briefly in a streak of sunlight, now casting green shadows against their bare arms.

A thin rain starts to fall. Lulled by the dreamy sounds and the caress of the drizzle, they shudder at the blast of a male orangutan's long-call. Starting on a low note, it whines higher and higher, then starts again on another note, and then again, until the series reaches a shrill crescendo four minutes later.

The humans are alert again. But Georgina does not stir in her nest. She is apparently unconcerned about the nearby adult orang which the humans recognize, by his call, as Nick, the resident male in the study area. The humans are curious about Georgina's attitude toward Nick. Because orangutans are almost antisocial, the times they meet to mate are of special interest. Galdikas is focusing this part of her study on orangutan mating and the connection—if there is one—between the animals that mate and the territory through which they travel. She is hoping to understand the way choosing a mate affects orangutan adaptation. When the orangutan separated from the common pongid ancestor eons ago, a unique process began that has resulted in dividing the living orang population into three distinct units: mothers and infants, adolescents, and solitary males. The units are incomplete because they must merge occasionally to perpetuate the species.

Georgina and Gale are typical of the first group—mothers and young children. Georgina will keep traveling through the rain forest with her small daughter for about four years, probably longer. The two may meet other mothers and infants from time to time, and pass a day or so foraging for food together. But little Gale will not get a chance to play with other youngsters very much. Her life will revolve around her mother and the inanimate objects in her forest world.

When Gale reaches four or five, Georgina will probably have another baby. By that time Gale will be weaned and able to feed herself and build her own nest. She will probably travel close to Georgina for several years, and she may spend her whole life in exactly the same few square miles as her mother.

But now, at less than a year, Gale still clings to Georgina constantly, as Sugito clung to Galdikas. Milk provides most of her nourishment, but once in a while she picks at the food her mother enjoys. Tasting her mother's crumbs and watching her select food, Gale will learn to forage for herself. Mother orangs never feed their children, but like gorillas, show them by example how to feed themselves.

Last week the observers watched two older mothers, Beth

and Cara, traveling with their children. These mothers meet often. But although they traveled together all day, they never touched and their infants did not really play *with* each other, as much as *alongside* each other, while their mothers ate.

Galdikas often sees four orangs—mothers and children—together. She has found as many as nine animals in one group. But when the number of animals is larger than five, tensions grow and the unstable group breaks up into smaller clusters again.

Little Gale likes to play as much as she can, but because she spends so much time hidden in the foliage, it is hard to know if she is making trial nests and trying to open fruits like Georgina. The humans can see her exercising her muscles, swinging from branches as daringly as any small gorilla. They have seen her tumbling with other infants, yet she does not enjoy the constant rough-and-ready play of small chimpanzees and gorillas. Even stranger, Gale does not get the chance to play the way the orangutan rehabs do at Camp Leakey.

When orangutans reach the age of four or five, the age of adolescence and subadulthood, they join up with their peers and form the next kind of social unit. The females stay adolescent until they have their first babies at the age of ten or eleven. Like the chimpanzees, they are sexually mature for several years before they become mothers and are accepted as full-fledged adults.

The males have a longer, more drawn-out adolescence and subadulthood, just like the male chimpanzees and gorillas. They become sexually active at the same time as their sisters. But it takes males until they are somewhere between twelve and fifteen to reach full size with complete cheek pads, beards, and the ability to sound the long-call. Thus, like the African apes, they must compete for some years with full-grown males before they become successful adults—if, indeed, they ever achieve success.

The female adolescents Fern and Maud used to be Georgina's closest companions before Gale's birth. Now Fern and Maud travel together. Galdikas has even seen them groom each other, which is not usual among orangutans. Mixed male and female pairs, like the female Noisy and her friend Mute, are also common. These mixed adolescent friendships seem to be just that, for the animals are not sexually interested in each other. Years ago natives of Borneo confused these small orangutans with the red leaf-eating monkeys. Both monkey and young ape are small and social in the way they stay together, unlike the adult orangutan, which is large and a loner.

Nick's powerful long-call pierces the forest again, and the observers turn their heads in the direction of the sound. Adult males like Nick make up the final unit of orangutans. Sullen giants, they live alone, avoiding all contact with each other. They emerge from their solitude only to mate. But when they show interest in a female, they confront each other and struggle furiously to keep their prize. Galdikas identifies the adult males by their battle scars and notes that she has not seen a single mature male unscathed. Some sport broken or stiff fingers, others are missing fingers altogether, while some have split lips or scars on their cheeks.

Galdikas suspects that these males are the winners. The others, she thinks, did not survive the battles and died beneath the trees in which they fought. She is convinced that these are battle scars and not inherited deformities, because neither the females nor the younger males are disfigured.

Maud and Fern thus are more likely than Mute to survive to reproduce their species. Right now the young females are teasing the observers, smacking their flexible lips and breaking off branches and twigs, which they hurl down. When they really want to put off intruders, they bombard them with larger fruits and heavy snags of trees. But they are habituated to these humans and are only playing.

Unlike gorillas, once they have accepted humans into their lives, they do not object to voices or any of the paraphernalia, the cameras and tape recorders, that the scientists bring along to record data. They allow Brindamour within three feet of them without seeking cover in the tall trees.

But Maud and Fern's antics disturbed Georgina. Still in her nest, she has just finished eating a purple flower and has begun to stretch her legs, one at a time, getting rid of all the kinks. Gale's small head peeks out over her mother's shoulder. Her huge, close-set round eyes dominate her tiny face, staring curiously at Maud and Fern.

Georgina is very protective of little Gale as she carefully grooms the soft red hair. Although Georgina grooms Gale frequently, she seldom grooms herself or any other orangutan. Finished, she climbs out of her nest and picks a dark egg-shaped fruit from an overhanging *rambutan* tree. She eats the meat sitting on a branch and sends the seeds, like pellets, to the ground, striking the observers on the head first.

Gale is still clinging to her mother's side hairs as Georgina climbs down about three feet and grabs another rambutan branch with both feet. Upside down, she picks more fruit with her hands and stuffs them into her mouth. Gale puts her hand out for a piece, but Georgina turns away. Mothers usually share their food with their infants, but occasionally they don't. The observers focus their binoculars. Gale's lips are back, exposing her small teeth in a sharp grimace. The scream that comes out from between those teeth, high-pitched and twangy, jangles the observers' nerves.

But not Georgina's. She ignores Gale's screams and continues eating. Gale is shaking her arms and legs now in the same kind of temper tantrum that infant African apes perform. But the orangutan mother does not react. The observers watch Gale exhaust herself screeching until she gives up and settles down beside her mother. Only then does Georgina turn and let Gale have some fruit, as though the tantrum had never happened. Her response to Gale's display is just the opposite from the way Fifi gave in to Freud. Gale sees the futility of such behavior, whereas Freud learned it as a successful way to get what he wanted.

Suddenly the observers see the branches sway dizzily as Maud and Fern add their weight to the slender tree. Georgina sees them but does not signal any greeting to these old chums. Orangs only seem to express emotion when they are frightened or sexually excited.

Two young orangutans fighting, above, and demonstrating the flexibility of their mouths when they "kiss."

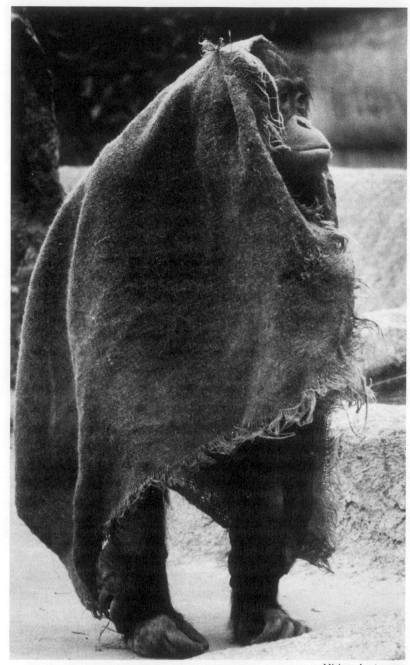

An orangutan will use any available material, here a piece of burlap, to cover its head.

Sexual dimorphism in orangutans is shown by the great size and weight of the mature male, with cheek pads and a throat pouch.

Rod Brindamour

Biruté Galdikas

Fern and Maud are slightly smaller than Georgina and are probably, at nine or ten, a year or so younger than she is. Because they are not yet mothers, they still behave as carefree adolescents. Before Gale's birth, Georgina was the same way. Fern and Maud peer curiously at little Gale. They show the same kind of "auntly" curiosity about the baby as young Fifi did when her chimp brother Flint was born, or young Flossie did toward the baby gorillas in Group Four. Fern and Maud poke their fingers in Gale's face. And that's enough for Georgina. She clicks her tongue in distress and pushes them away.

She leaves her old friends, preferring to be alone with Gale. Perhaps when Fern and Maud have babies, they will all be companions again and meet up once in a while as Beth and Cara do, spending whole days together with their infants. But for now, Georgina moves into the next tree. She does not swing, but reaches out with her long arms and grabs the slender trunk. This brachiating movement is very beautiful. Rod Brindamour has caught it on film in its full grace. Using three of her four limbs, because orangutans' feet are as agile as their hands, Georgina rocks the tree from side to side, setting up a pendulum motion. With each swing, the pliant tree moves in a greater arc until at last Georgina can lean over and transfer her body to the next tree.

Orangutans are the heaviest of all arboreal animals and they fall frequently. The lucky ones manage to grab a branch as they plummet by, but many crash all the way to the humus-covered soil, especially the heavier males (which is another possible reason for their twisted toes and fingers).

Nervous for little Gale, the humans watch Georgina as she continues moving at a right angle to the direction that Fern and Maud are taking. Then the humans confer, check the compasses that each of them carries, and split up. One will follow Georgina and baby Gale; the other will keep up with the adolescent females. Neither moves far. Female orangs seldom cover more than two miles a day and never leave the six square miles of their home area throughout their lives. Female ranges overlap so much that they cannot claim any private territory. The male orangutans move farther afield, but how far is still unknown.

Nick's long-call sounds very close. This time Georgina responds by accelerating her flight. The long-call seems to do several things: it attracts some females and at the same time warns both females and males to get out of the way because a mature male is nearby. It is also the sound males make when mating. As Georgina moves, Gale slips down and her high-pitched whimper hangs in the moist air. Georgina pauses briefly, hoists Gale up on her side, then keeps on moving so fast that below her, the observer has to run to keep apace. Young mothers like Georgina actively evade adult males until their infants are large enough to get along independently and they are ready to have another child.

At last Nick comes into view, not in the trees, but moving four-legged along the ground, as Galdikas had first observed in 1971. They only climb into the trees to eat and sleep, but even that is not essential. Galdikas has seen a subadult male bend a sapling down as a pillow, and nap on the ground for three quarters of an hour.

Nick moves slowly into the lower branches of the *banitan* tree, plucking fruit to eat as he moves on. He almost collides with another pair of adolescents, the female Noisy and her friend Mute. As fast as Georgina scurried off, Noisy dashes toward Nick, attracted by his call.

At eight years of age, Noisy is sexually mature and seems to be in estrus, ready to mate. Like a gorilla, she gives no visible sign, but reveals her state by flirtatious gestures. Noisy climbs down to a branch alongside Nick's, then edges toward the imposing cheek-flapped figure and crouches, turning her rump toward Nick's face. She is letting him know that she is anxious to mate.

Meanwhile, Mute has retreated. He is about fifty yards away in another tree, peeking at his companions from a hide of branches. At the moment, however, there is very little to see. Nick had begun eating a banitan, a favored fruit that looks like a globe and contains two very hard pits. Inside each pit there is a minute portion of sweet-tasting meat that is, to an orangutan, at least, worth the hours of effort he has to spend crushing the pits with his teeth to get them open.

Noisy is not as interested in the banitan as she is in Nick, and tries to distract him. She solicits him with her rump, then runs her fingers through his long red hair, grooming him as a female chimpanzee might court a male—a rare gesture from an orangutan. Nick does not repel her, but he goes on chewing his pit.

Suddenly, in a gesture that surprises Nick, as well as the observer, Noisy throws her arms around Nick's neck and hugs him. This seems to convince Nick. Finally, after spitting out the last of the pit and chewing the sweet center, he condescends to mate with her. The observer cannot see them clearly through the thick foliage, but he can hear Nick's familiar long-call, now a song of mating.

Nick moves away now, alone. Noisy rejoins Mute, who settles down with her to work on some banitans of their own. Except for mating, Noisy clearly prefers Mute's company to the more sexually mature Nick. Month after month she has sought out Nick when she comes into estrus; he is the only resident mature male in the study area now.

But not the only male. Galdikas has observed other adult males roaming the forests and swamp. When these transients find a female in estrus, they follow her, sometimes successfully mate with her, then disappear. Resident males like Nick stay in one place for several years and choose a female with whom they spend the several days each month that she is in estrus, in what ethologists call a "consort relationship." Some consorts even remain with their females while they are pregnant.

When the Brindamours arrived at the Tanjung Puting Reserve in 1971, Nick was not living there. But T.P., with his abnormally inflated laryngeal sac, was easy to recognize. He was the first wild orangutan who allowed them to watch him. At the time he was consorting with Priscilla, a young mother with a small son, Pug. Eventually, however, Priscilla became pregnant again, probably with T.P.'s infant, which was born nine months after the Brindamours observed them mating. But before the baby arrived, T.P. disappeared. It was not until seven months later that Nick appeared and, with no apparent opposition, took over the territory.

Now Nick has left the banitan tree to Noisy and Mute. The observer has been leaning against the trunk waiting for them to finish their work on the hard pits, when a crashing sound indicates a struggle in the canopy. The observer looks up to see Noisy, who just a while ago was so anxious to mate with Nick, struggling frantically with a subadult male barely larger than herself, who has only the first signs of cheek pads on his face. The male ape knows she is in estrus and intends to mate with her whether she wants to or not.

The turmoil sends down a hail of branches, twigs, and leaves, as if a cyclone were whipping through the trees. Noisy is fighting off the ardent young male, but he is bigger and stronger and attacks her from behind, pins her down on the sturdy branch, and mates. The low grunts that Noisy utters are the ugliest vocalizations that the observer has ever recorded. It is a sound only heard from females being sexually assaulted. Getting it down on tape, the disagreeable wail blends dissonantly with the attacker's hapless effort to make a long-call. He cannot yet complete it, just as he cannot yet win a female's voluntary compliance.

Noisy's behavior does not surprise the observer. It fits the pattern Galdikas has discerned, in which adolescent orangutans of both sexes are anxious to mate with mature animals, and just as anxious to avoid sexual encounters with their peers. Rapes like this are relatively frequent among these unsocial primates, where all events are infrequent on a human social scale. But from what the Brindamours have observed, the females do not seem to become pregnant after these assaults. It is as if the process of selection ensures that only the larger males who have successfully won a female will father the next generation.

Noisy recovers and joins Mute again. They are both still small enough to travel easily through the canopy's branches. Half an hour later, Noisy and Mute come to a tree where an older female orang, Beth, and her small daughter are eating. Mute, who had stood by curiously watching Noisy's ordeal, now assaults Beth, who is just as unwilling to mate with him as Noisy was to mate with her assailant. But Beth has an ally in her fight—her child. They both fling out their arms at Mute, scratching and biting him with all their might. It looks as if the two of them may fend him off, until Noisy joins the melee on Mute's side. Below, the tape recorder picks up the same low guttural sound from Beth that Noisy uttered earlier in the morning. With her child following, Beth finally escapes, leaving Mute and Noisy resting in a patch of light that dapples their hair with orange highlights.

The observer realizes that the sun is at its zenith; the heat evaporates the drizzle into a steamy cloud that rises from the ground to blur the edges of the green leaves and flowering lianas that decorate the tropical rain forest.

Afternoon

Noisy and Mute sit comfortably in the arms of a *durian* tree, ready to stuff themselves with the luscious custardy meat of the spiky, green, football-sized fruit. Although the durian exude a stench like rotted flesh, the sweet flavor makes it a luxury food in Chinese and Indonesian markets, as well as among the orangutans. Noisy picks a large fruit with her hands, then carries it in her mouth to a broad branch. She sits down to split it open, hungry for the twelve chestnut-sized seeds inside. She eats them greedily, heaving the rind down to the forest floor.

Orangutans are frugivorous, preferring fruit to all other foods. But they also eat flowers, leaves, eggs, and insects. Other observers beyond the Tanjung Puting Reserve have even seen them raiding beehives for honey. But during lean years, such as the one that followed the Brindamours' first season in Borneo, the orangs resorted to chewing bark, often killing saplings. When the drought continued, males like T.P. wandered off, leaving the less adventuresome females behind. Galdikas observes that the total orangutan population really depends on how many apes the forest can feed during its worst seasons, as well as how often the females have babies.

At last Noisy and Mute begin to grow drowsy. Like the African apes, they take an afternoon nap and build themselves nests in which to sleep. Sixty feet off the ground, the nests are sturdy, several yards apart in the same tree. Noisy finds a fork in the boughs near the trunk, and reaches out to bend some nearby branches. She selects one slim branch from above her head, breaks it, and eats the leaves off before she inserts the bare stick into her nest. This is about all the tool-making that has been noticed among free-ranging orangutans.

Noisy breaks off more branches, turning slowly as she works. Because she is moving in a circle, the branches tend to weave together. But the weaving seems to be accidental, a result of her movements. Finishing up, she fills the center with some cushioning leaves and lets a single branch stick out, like a handle. She hesitates, then pulls herself out by one arm and grabs a small fruit to take back with her for a snack. Returning to her nest, she grabs the handle branch and uses it to pivot back inside.

Finished, at least for the moment, Noisy is settling down when the drizzle turns into a downpour. Up she climbs and, without any delay, makes a second platform over her head. Orangutans dislike rain as much as the African apes, but orangs do something about it. When they cannot find shelter naturally, they make a roof platform to protect themselves.

Mute is less ambitious, and in a leafier part of the tree. He does not build a roof, but instead breaks off a leafy branch and holds it up, like an umbrella. The observer below covers the tape recorder, which is filled with silica gel to prevent rust, then pulls out a raincoat.

The orangutans will sleep for about three hours in the steady rain. The observers signal with their whistles and meet. They compare notes, collect specimens of what the orangutans have eaten, and take shelter from the downpour beneath a betel palm tree. They decide to remain together to see what Noisy and Mute are up to. And they get back to the durian tree in plenty of time to see the young animals wake up.

The rain has stopped, leaving a small pool of water in a hollow beside Mute's nest. Sitting up, Mute cups his hand and dips it into the hollow. Most of the water runs off, but Mute sucks the droplets from his long red hair, puckering up his lips and making a sucking sound that the humans can hear below. Then he climbs down to the spongy earth, with Noisy trailing him. The humans follow them through the muddy forest.

Mute, a subadult, has encountered only females and infants today, except when Noisy solicited Nick. Then Mute prudently remained well out of sight. Hungry, however, for variety in his menu, Mute discovers a wet log glistening on the ground and breaks off a small branch, inspecting it for termites. Suddenly he discovers Nick, huge old Nick, carefully eating termites at the other end. Mute is more fearful than hungry; his hairs stand on end as he drops the wood and scampers off with Noisy on all fours.

The observers wait to see Nick eating termites. They are curious to see if he will try to use a tool as some people had reported witnessing elsewhere on the island. But he just breaks off pieces of wood and inspects them with his fingers. One of the humans sits down about six feet from Nick on the other end of the log. Too close. Nick stops and turns. Standing up on his rear legs, he advances on the frightened human until he is less than an arm's length away. Terrified, the observer avoids looking directly into Nick's eyes—a universal sign of aggression among the great apes—and, head down, moves slowly, very slowly, still crouching, and slips off the log onto the ground, then waits.

After what seems like a very long time, Nick retreats to his own end of the log and continues eating termites. He is not particularly violent or aggressive and is habituated to these people. He simply rejected the idea of sharing his termite supply. Out of danger, the observers remember another close call from T.P. during their first year in the field. The occasion was even more alarming.

The Brindamours were new to the forest then, and everywhere they went young Sugito accompanied them, clinging to his stepmother's shoulders most of the time, but daring, as he grew curious, to explore the higher branches of the green canopy when they stopped to observe the wild animals. One day he spotted T.P. eating in a tree. Sugito was used to playing with humans and the other rehabs at Camp Leakey, so he expected T.P. to play with him as well. T.P. did not appear to notice little Sugito at first, so the infant tried to attract his attention. He succeeded, only to learn that free-ranging adult orangutans are not the same as captive juveniles. T.P. raged at the small animal, chasing him straight down the tree trunk into Galdikas's arms.

When she looked up, T.P. had followed Sugito down to within a body length of the top of her head. She just backed away, ready to run for it with Sugito in her arms and an enraged T.P. at her heels. Happily, Brindamour kept cool. He raised his machete blade while staring directly into T.P.'s eyes, and then chopped down a young tree in a gesture that dared T.P. to do something about it. T.P. retreated higher in the branches, sounding an angry bellow from above.

Adult male orangutans, unlike male chimpanzees and gorillas, seem intolerant of infants. This is probably because they are not part of the family unit. Mothers do not fear any predators and do not need the protection that male animals usually provide. Orangutan fathers never develop the solicitude that gorillas and chimpanzees show when their youngsters use their bodies as slides and jungle gyms.

Male orangs use their time differently from the females. They spend more hours eating because they are bigger and need more food. Nick stays termiting for a while and carefully breaks off pieces, sucking out the juicy insects. Males eat many more termites than the females, perhaps because they spend more time on the ground.

Finally Nick is sated and he moves out of the forest into the swamp. Tall reeds grow right down into the water, camouflaging where land ends and water begins. Nick plows ahead, wading waist deep. Unlike the chimps and the gorillas, he does not mind the water, although he cannot swim. His red hair darkens as he submerges. But when the river gets too deep, he steps onto a log and balances across on it, surprisingly agile for such a heavy animal. The humans follow, holding their equipment above their heads, snug in high boots. They note that the river can have nothing to do with confining the orangutan to its range.

Out of the swamp, they follow Nick into another section of dry forest. Then they all pause, Nick and the humans. A stranger's long-call rings out, almost on top of them. The humans peer up at the backs of a large male and female orangutan, and they wonder how Nick will respond to them.

Three years ago, when T.P. reigned over the territory and was consorting with Priscilla, a newcomer confronted him and the humans witnessed a fierce struggle among the high branches. For twenty minutes the males grappled, biting the exposed parts of hands, shoulders, and faces. Over and over again they plummeted to the ground and climbed back up, determined to continue fighting. Breathless, they would pause, and move back upon their branches, panting heavily, never taking their eyes from one another. During these pauses each male would break off heavy snags, heaving them noisily to the ground. Finally, the stranger retreated, leaving the battlefield redolent with orangutan smell for a long while afterward.

Today Nick stares at the consorting couple, then breaks off a snag and tosses it. The consorting pair know he is there and move rapidly away together, brachiating through the branches.

Nick wanders off on the ground. The humans think about returning to Camp Dart before night falls. Suddenly a familiar long-call echoes in the distance, perhaps three quarters of a mile away. Their eyebrows rise. They recognize the call of T.P., who had returned as unheralded as he had disappeared two years earlier. Not having seen him for two years, they had assumed him dead, until they saw his familiar distended throat pouch again on April Fool's Day 1974. Since then they have heard his long-call often in the territory.

Days pass. The observers continue their patrol, documenting the lives of the habituated animals. Orangutans live slowly and their behavioral pattern is subtle. Months and years replace the old time-scale of days and weeks before revelations begin to unfold.

Galdikas guessed T.P. had come home because of an abundant crop of fruit throughout the forest, and perhaps because Priscilla was ready to have another baby and T.P. had been her consort. But she was only partly right. T.P. is enjoying the fruit, but he has begun to court another female. It is not Priscilla, but Val whom he has chosen.

T.P. and Val's consortship lasts several days, during which they avoid all other orangutans, eat in the same trees, and nest near each other at night. Once in a while they observe Val grooming T.P. But they never see him reciprocate. They keep company this way for three whole days, but they do not mate until the fourth day. When they do, they climb high into the canopy and hook their feet onto overhead supporting branches. T.P. reclines on a broad branch with Val on top of him. They are the only primates, besides humans, who face each other when they mate. As in the other matings the observers have witnessed, T.P.'s long-call broadcasts his success to the forest.

For a while the reserve seems to teem with adult male orangs, perhaps because the food supply is rich, perhaps because more than one female is ready to mate. T.P. remained interested in Val and sought her out month after month. Nick is still there too, sharing the territory for a while with T.P. and now actively seeking out Noisy, for her sexual appeal has apparently grown as she matured.

T.P.'s return after mysteriously disappearing proves that long-range research is crucial to understanding such private primates. Already Galdikas has confirmed earlier sightings that described orangs as not entirely arboreal apes, and she has watched them spending whole days on the forest floor. She has also calculated that these admittedly solitary creatures spend almost 18 percent of their waking hours within sight of others of their species.

Her observations have not toppled the earlier image of the red-haired introvert. But she has certainly modified it and fleshed out the skeletal picture of orangutan life.

Night falls as she climbs into Camp Dart. Lighting the kerosene lamp, Galdikas begins to jot down her observations. T.P.'s long-call pierces the night, and he is answered immediately by

Nick. A third long-call picks up the cry and Galdikas pauses. Three long-calls together—a new phenomenon. What does it mean? She notes it down and leaves some space. She and Rod Brindamour will stay here at Tanjung Puting Reserve indefinitely. One day she hopes to fill in all the blanks.

CONCLUSION

Leakey's Legacy

Earl's Court Road, a clutter of shoppers and shops in the heart of London, is worlds away from Leakey's dry gorge at Olduvai or the rain forests of Tanzania, Rwanda, and Borneo. Yet it was in an old-fashioned English apartment here, on a fall evening in 1971, that Louis Leakey finally hosted all three of his protégé primatologists together. He enjoyed every moment of it. The chimpanzee project had already won international acclaim; the gorilla study was well under way; and the Brindamours were in England, en route from California to Indonesia with a plan to habituate the orangutan. That evening turned out to be the only time they would all meet. Several months later Leakey died, without having visited any of the projects he had worked so hard to start.

When Leakey sent Jane Goodall to the shores of Lake Tanganyika in 1960, he did not know what he was starting. Ethology was not his main concern. He was interested in paleontology and human evolution, and he suspected that the Gombe chimps, which were reputed to spend a lot of time on the lakeshores, might give some clue to the lives of the early hominids, those long-dead creatures whose fossils he was digging up in ancient lake sites.

Leakey was familiar enough with chimpanzees to spot the parallels between their behavior and ours. He hoped that the

Gombe group would prove to be a "missing-chimp-link," a group of apes in the process of adapting to an open space, like the African savanna was millions of years ago when *Australopithecus* emerged from the forests.

Leakey wanted women to do this work. He liked women and had a way of stimulating their self-confidence. He helped male students too, but at a time when it was not as acceptable to encourage female scientists, he sought out interested young women and helped them get established.

He chose them because he had an almost mystical faith in what he called "feminine qualities" that had nothing whatever to do with the modern movement for equality. He believed that women are more sensitive and gentler than men, perhaps because of their role as nurturers. These attributes, he suspected, would enable them to establish rapport with wild animals. Leakey's choice of Goodall, and later Fossey and Galdikas, proved to him that he was right. He never talked of the many other women he had supported who had not succeeded. His choice of these three scientists proved wise, not necessarily because they are women, but because they are exceptionally courageous, perceptive, and patient individuals.

As time went on, Leakey appreciated the popular response to Goodall's work, and he was clever enough as a fund-raiser to appeal to the romance of the jungle-girl, an image as old as Tarzan's Jane, to keep the projects going. Expanding on his choice of female scientists, he argued convincingly that they had an advantage over male ethologists because they could win the affection of the young apes without provoking hostility from the adult males.

Leakey also had the right idea about studying chimpanzees. The Gombe group, though slightly different from other chimps, had not learned to swim or perform unchimp-like skills. They are not a bridge between chimp and man. But Jane Goodall's remarkable description of their behavior has greatly stimulated the study of animal behavior and given new life to several scientific disciplines, including Leakey's own interest—the study of human evolution.

The real difference between primatology and all the other kinds of ethology in which scientists observe fish and birds and elephants is that we share with chimps not only the structures of our skeletons, enzymes, and brains, but behavioral patterns that we have probably retained from our common hominoid ancestor. The patterns that Goodall perceived in the chimpanzee social system strike us by their familiarity.

Chimpanzees, and to a lesser degree gorillas and orangutans, groom each other for more than simple hygienic reasons. In grooming they express respect, affection, and reassurance. It is easy to see how grooming gradually changed into caresses and kisses when the human primate somehow, in a way that no one has yet explained, lost most of its body hair. Likewise, the chimpanzee's play-face, teeth bared, lips wide and pulled back, gradually became the human smile. Chimps even grin in the same situations as humans—when they are happy and when they are uneasy.

Chimpanzees and gorillas instinctively duck their heads to avoid low-flying birds; orangutans make covers for their heads. And humans duck to avoid low-flying objects, wear hats, and use umbrellas. When Goodall confronted a chimpanzee in the forest with a full-length mirror, he clutched his companion in alarm, in the same way a person grabs a friend at a scary movie. It is just as easy to identify man's earliest tool-making and hunting efforts with the Gombe chimps. But the actual connections between our ancestors and the chimps is not known. It is hard to see what kind of evidence can show up—short of new fossil discoveries that go far beyond present ones—which can make these ideas more than provocative speculations.

Yet these same data are extraordinarily effective when they are used to parallel today's chimpanzee behavior with ours. For decades medical researchers have used apes to test drugs and new surgical techniques. Now psychiatrists and psychologists are using chimpanzees as stand-ins for human behavioral disorders. Flo's intense mothering, Figan and Faben's brotherly solidarity, and Flint's tragic grief show that certain fundamental emotional reactions are common to man and chimp.

When Leakey saw the importance of this aspect of Goodall's research, he suspected that a comparison between the adaptation of the chimpanzees to their environment and the adaptations of the other great apes to theirs might reveal more about all hominoid behavior, including the human primate. The gorilla and orangutan studies are still in preliminary stages compared to the chimpanzee research. Already, however, striking similarities, as well as contrasts, have appeared.

All the apes look alike, with hairy torsos, short legs, and long arms. When they are small they all brachiate, but they prefer to move along the ground on all fours when they mature. In grasslands, where they all travel some of the time, they can stand bipedally to see over the tall grasses. But they prefer the forests. Even though the chimpanzees and gorillas are almost completely terrestrial in travel, they depend on trees for most of their food and for shelter at night. Nomads, they build new nests to sleep in each evening and rise with the sun to spend the day traveling in search of food, except for one long, midday siesta.

Within these confines, however, they lead very different lives. A boisterous, excitable chimpanzee knows at least thirty other chimps and communicates with them through a wide repertoire of postures, gestures, facial expressions, and sounds. The lethargic gorilla knows a smaller group and lives at a much slower pace. The events that happen in one chimpanzee day might take months to happen in a gorilla group. Finally, the solitary orangutan largely avoids his peers altogether and, what takes months to happen among gorillas might take years with the free-ranging orangutans.

Within the species, each study group is different. And within the study groups, each animal is special. Years ago, when primate ethology was scarcely a science at all, a glimpse of one gorilla or a pair of chimpanzees was enough for an expert to declare that all chimpanzees eat honey, or that all orangutans are arboreal. Goodall's studies show that her Gombe chimps termite and hunt, but they do not smash fruit with stones as other chimps have been reported to do. Likewise, Galdikas's Borneo orangs move on the ground, while their cousins on Sumatra, which still boasts wild tigers, stay aloft. Within the groups, strong personalities, like the chimpanzee Flo, influence many of the other animals around them, the way that a gorilla silverback, like Rafiki, sets the tone for his whole group.

The impact of individuals is a sign of the crucial role that learning plays in primates. The more highly developed an animal, the more individual the members of the species. This is because the higher primates are born helpless and depend on the experiences of their early years to shape their intelligence.

Next to humans, the great apes spend more time completely dependent on an adult than any other animal. Like ourselves, the apes are born with an innate curiosity that makes them want to learn certain skills. All of these studies show the close connection between innate abilities, which can be seen as hereditary, and learning, the influence of their environment. These are not distinct influences, as biologists once believed. It seems that an animal inherits the tendency to want to learn certain things. Whether or not an ape, or a young human, learns, depends on what models it sees. For example, only Gombe chimps termite the way they do because at Gombe the mother chimp demonstrates the skill for her child. Another chimp could probably learn termiting if a Gombe mother were to raise it. In other parts of Africa, chimps have been seen using rocks and sticks as tools. But a young gorilla would probably not learn to termite, even if it could be adopted by a chimp mother. There probably is nothing in a gorilla's genetic structure that predisposes it to tool-using.

All the apes are eager to learn, but for the most part they accept only one teacher in their early years—their mothers. Unlike human children, who are raised not only by mothers, but by fathers and grandparents and even baby sitters, the small ape is not so flexible. Should an ape be orphaned within its first two years, when it is totally dependent on its mother, it seldom survives in the wild. And even when it loses its mother later, but while still a juvenile, it remains stunted emotionally for the rest of its life.

Mother apes show their children by example what to eat and how to build a nest. They also demonstrate for them the social codes of the group, and especially among chimpanzees and gorillas, respect for the male hierarchy. Mother orangutans, which do not discipline their children to follow rules, seem to show them by example how to avoid all other orangutans except when they want to mate.

All the great apes have approximately the same life-span in the wild, about thirty-five years (although there is no precise data for any of them), and they spend nearly the same length of time in the early, crucial stages of development. These stages include infancy, when they learn acceptable emotional expres-sions, and adolescence. The newborn ape needs physical contact and nourishment from its mother, and responds by snuggling up to her breast. When it is deprived of this comfort, it becomes angry and frustrated, flailing out in a temper tantrum. Chimp and gorilla mothers inadvertently reward these displays by giving in to them. According to Dr. David Hamburg, a colleague of Goodall's at Stanford, these tantrums grow into the great dis-plays of ground-thumping, branch-breaking, and chest-pounding that characterize adult males. The orangutan infant, ignored when it rages, does not seem to develop such ritualized emotional displays for courting or competing with other males. When the orangutan is forced into a confrontation with another animal, he fights for real.

Adolescence is the second great learning period for apes, and, of course, for humans too. These are the years when the young animal is most friendly with its peers. It leaves its mother alto-gether, or if it is a chimpanzee, for great stretches of time. Even the orangutan is sociable at this stage. These are the years when it learns to mate—conveniently remaining sterile for a while if it is a female chimp or orang. A female chimp or gorilla will seek out small animals to play with, apprenticing in child-care. This may be a time of frustration for the female orang, since observations show that she might like to explore babies more than she is allowed.

Adolescence and subadulthood are different for the males of all three species. African apes have to struggle for a position within the hierarchy and at the same time compete with other males for females. The orangutan, it appears, spends these years learning to live in solitude and at the same time struggling to win females from the larger, more sexually attractive males.

At first glance, the chimpanzees seem the cleverest of the apes, the gorillas next, and last of all the orangutans. This was the order in which primatologists rated them fifty years ago. Recent laboratory tests done on captive apes, geared to rate their comparative intelligence, do not corroborate this theory. The outgoing chimpanzee, the familial gorilla, and the lone orangutan achieve similar scores, although the orangutan outperforms the others.

Captive chimpanzees and gorillas have been taught to communicate with sign language, but they do not string abstract ideas together. Gorillas, on the other hand, which cannot use tools, excel in memory and in identifying abstract symbols. The orangutan outperforms the others in using a tool and in making another tool for a different purpose. Most of these current experiments use young apes. Even circuses discard their performing chimpanzees after they mature. Sexual maturity somehow affects an ape's ability to use its intelligence.

The laboratory tests are perplexing. But they are not as difficult to understand as the peculiar behavior of the orangutan and how it fits into overall primate behavior. It used to be assumed that, as primates developed, they lived in more and more complex societies, approaching, as they evolved, the order of human society. It seemed obvious that social behavior evolved as a companion to intelligence, and that groups of chimpanzees and gorillas organize themselves around dominant males the way human societies organize themselves around leaders and chieftains.

But the orangutan, with its obvious intelligence and a physiology which, if not as close to ours as the chimpanzee's, is close enough, upsets this assumption. The orang uses its intelligence more to avoid intimate social contact than to seek it out. In this case something besides simple intelligence seems to determine why a species develops a social system.

A possible explanation of the orangutans' relative solitude versus the African apes' amiability is the difference in their forest habitats. Professor Peter Rodman of the University of California at Davis suggests a three-way equation. He says that two separate factors correlate with the degree of sociability of the apes. The factors are its diet and the degree of its sexual dimorphism. Chimps eat fruit, a food that is relatively hard to get and for which the animals compete. But chimps are not sexually dimorphic, so that the males and females eat the same quantities and can live together as social creatures.

Gorillas eat leafy foods, which are plentiful, and therefore, even though gorillas are sexually dimorphic, they are still sociable because they do not have to compete for food. But the orangutan is both a fruit eater and sexually dimorphic. This means that the males must find private food trees and spend more time in them filling up, compared with females, which makes for antisocial apes. Rodman supports this theory with the added information that orangutans do not have any predators, so that the females do not need the males to protect their infants. And he caps it by saying that this ecological formula is equally valid for a two-inch-tall prosimian, a primate called the *Galago demidovii,* or African bush baby, which lives in Gabon, West Africa, in incomplete social units just like the orangutan.

This is a fascinating explanation of the family structure of orangutans. But it still leaves unanswered their lack of manual ingenuity in the wild, compared to their skills at Camp Leakey and in the primate laboratory. Nor does it explain why active infants in all of the species become somber adults.

The first step toward a complete understanding will emerge from the work of Goodall, Fossey, and Galdikas. Remaining aloof from their subjects so that they will not bias their insights by projecting human motives on the animals, they are describing, in detail, the way the apes live as an organic part of their natural habitats. The next step would be large, outdoor, controlled facilities for gorillas and orangutans as there now are for chimpanzees. We might then learn more about the specific effects of hormones on behavior and on learning.

Behind all of these primate studies, even though some of the scientists who are doing them may not agree, there is a special fascination with the great apes because there, but for the roll of the genetic dice, is man. A young Congolese who accompanied Fossey during her African safari expressed it for all of us when, awed at the sight of his first gorilla, he whispered, "Surely, Lord, these are our relations."

INDIVIDUAL CHARACTERISTICS

	Arboreal/ Terrestrial	Sexual Dimorphism	Movement	Nest-building / Tool-using	Water	Diet
Chimpanzee	Spends time in trees and on ground	Not especially dimorphic Males only slightly larger than females	Four-legged in trees with some brachiation On ground often bipedal for short distances	In trees _Make crude tools_	Avoids being in but drinks	Mostly frugivorous Also eats insects and some meat and bark
Gorilla	Mostly on ground, but climbs into trees for fruit and sometimes to sleep	Sexually dimorphic Males much larger and develop white hair along back with age	Four-legged in trees On ground bipedal for short distances	In trees and on ground _No tools_	Avoids being in and does not drink	Mostly herbivorous Eats some fruit, insects, and snails
Orangutan	Mostly in trees, but males travel on ground and come down to eat termites in fallen trees	Sexually dimorphic Males twice as large as females and develop cheek pads, throat pouches, and sometimes beards	Four-legged in trees with some brachiation On ground rarely bipedal	In trees and sometimes with "roof" _No tools_	Wades through and also drinks	Frugivorous Also eats some insects and bark

GROUP CHARACTERISTICS

	Size and Composition	Dominance Hierarchy	Interaction Between Groups	Grooming Between Adults
Chimpanzee	Community of about 30, but individuals move about in subgroups from 2 to 15 members Contains many males, females, and infants which constantly break up and then rearrange themselves in smaller groups	Males dominant over most females Within males there is an Alpha male who is dominant	Frequent peaceful mixing within community Tension and fighting when in competition with another community	Great deal of mutual grooming, inter- and intra-sexual Heavy grooming when female in estrus Adult males groom each other extensively
Gorilla	Groups vary from 5 to 17, but average group has 12 members Each group has dominant male, subordinate younger males, adult females, and young	Males dominant with linear hierarchy led by silverback	Peaceful, slow communication in own group Aggressive displays and occasional fighting between groups	Occasional female grooming of male Almost never the reverse or male-male grooming
Orangutan	No enduring groups Adult females and 1 or 2 infants may meet with other similar group Adolescents may move in groups of 2 or 3	No hierarchy, but single resident male seems to preside over home range	Rare intimate communication between groups, but some; adolescents mix more than adults Adult males fight over female in estrus Adult male long-call important in communication	Seldom seen except by female in estrus grooming male Adult males do not groom each other

COMMUNICATION

	Vocalizations	Facial Expressions	Postures	Displays
Chimpanzee	Communicates using wide variety of different sounds, which are responded to by other members of community	Many facial expressions, several play-face smiles and frowns	Bowing and turning of rump indicates submission as well as sexual receptivity Head-patting and reassurance touching	Great ritualized emotional outbursts among males in competition for place in hierarchy and in courting females
Gorilla	Communicates using wide variety of different sounds Silverback vocalizes most, females least Most vocalization between group members, and receive response Also used by silverbacks of different groups to keep groups apart	Play-face and frown, but not as varied as chimpanzee	Submissive crouch for sexual receptivity Cuffing as rebuke	Ritualized chest-beating and noisy display between males and to ward off other animals
Orangutan	Very few vocalizations Vocalizations not answered, but used as one-way emotional expressions Males use long-call to attract females and warn off other males	Seems to retain poker face in wild Play-face and wide variety of expressions in captivity	Not observed	Only when courting or to frighten off intruders

Bibliography

All of the material listed below contributed to this book. Much of it, however, is inaccessible to the general reader. Of those works that are available, I recommend especially the books and magazine articles that are preceded by an asterisk (*).

Bourne, Geoffrey H. *The Ape People*. New York: G. P. Putnam's Sons, 1971.

* ———. *Primate Odyssey*. New York: G. P. Putnam's Sons, 1974.

* Cole, Sonia. *Leakey's Luck*. New York: Harcourt Brace Jovanovich, 1975.

DeVore, Irven, ed. *Primate Behavior: Field Studies of Monkeys and Apes*. New York: Holt, Rinehart and Winston, 1965.

DeVore, Irven and Eimerl, Sarel. *The Primates*. New York: Time-Life Books, 1965.

Dolhinow, Phyllis, ed. *Primate Patterns*. New York: Holt, Rinehart and Winston, 1972. See particularly the chapters by S. L. Washburn and David A. Hamburg, "Aggressive Behavior in Old World Monkeys and Apes" and "Evolution of Primate Behavior."

Du Chaillu, Paul B. *Explorations and Adventures in Equatorial Africa*. London: John Murray, 1861.

Fossey, Dian. "One Girl's Safari," *Louisville Courier-Journal,* July 19, 1964.

———. "I Photographed the Mountain Gorilla," *Louisville Courier-Journal,* July 26, 1964.

* ———. "Making Friends with Mountain Gorillas," *National Geographic,* January 1970.

* ———. "More Years with Mountain Gorillas," *National Geographic,* October 1971.

———. "Vocalizations of the Mountain Gorilla," *Animal Behaviour,* Vol. 20, 1972.

———. "Observations on the Home Range of One Group of Mountain Gorillas (Gorilla Gorilla Berengei)," *Animal Behaviour,* Vol. 22, 1974.

Galdikas, Biruté F. "Orangutan Adaptation at Tanjung Puting Reserve: Mating and Ecology," for Burg Wartenstein Symposium, N. 62.

* ———. "Orangutans, Indonesia's 'People of the Forest,' " *National Geographic,* October 1975.

Garner, Robert Lynch. *Apes and Monkeys.* Boston: Ginn and Co., 1900.

Groves, Colin P. *Gorillas.* New York: Arco Publishing Co., 1970.

Hamburg, David A. "Crowding, Stranger Contact, and Aggressive Behavior." In *Society, Stress and Disease,* Vol. 1. Lennart Levi, ed. New York: Oxford University Press, 1971.

Hamburg, David A. and van Lawick-Goodall, Jane. "Chimpanzee Behavior as a Model of the Behavior of Early Man." In *American Handbook of Psychiatry: New Psychiatric Frontiers,* Vol. 6. David A. Hamburg and H. Keith H. Brodie, eds. New York: Basic Books, 1974.

Harrisson, Barbara. *Orang-Utan,* New York: Doubleday, 1963.

* van Lawick-Goodall, Jane. *My Friends the Wild Chimpanzees.* Washington, D.C.: National Geographic Society, 1967.

* ———. *In the Shadow of Man.* Boston: Houghton Mifflin, 1971.

van Lawick-Goodall, Jane and Hamburg, David A. "A Proposal for Temporary Support of Basic Operations at the Gombe Stream Research Center," 1973.

———. "Gombe East, Gombe West," *The Stanford Magazine,* Spring/Summer 1974, Vol. 2/1.

L. S. B. Leakey Foundation. "In Search of Man: Some Questions and Answers in African Archeology and Primatology," Los Angeles, 1974.

MacKinnon, John. *In Search of the Red Ape.* New York: Holt, Rinehart and Winston, 1974.

Morris, Desmond, ed. *Primate Ethology.* Chicago: Aldine, 1974.

Rodman, Peter Stevens. "Synecology of Bornean Primates With Special Reference to the Behavior of the Ecology of Orang Utans," Harvard University, Ph.D. thesis in Biological Anthropology, 1973.

Rumbaugh, Duane M. "Learning Skills of Anthropoids." In *Primate Behavior, Developments in Field and Laboratory Research,* Vol. 1. Leonard A. Rosenblum, ed. New York: Academic Press, 1970.

Ruwet, Jean-Claud. *Introduction to Ethology, The Biology of Behavior.* New York: International Universities Press, 1972.

* Schaller, George B. *The Year of the Gorilla.* Chicago: University of Chicago Press, 1964.

Simonds, Paul E. *The Social Primates.* New York: Harper & Row, 1974.

Yerkes, Robert M. and Ada W. *The Great Apes: A Study of Anthropoid Life.* New Haven: Yale University Press, 1929.

Index

Italic number indicates photograph